SCHOLARSHIP AND POLITICS IN SOUTH AFRICA'S HIGHER EDUCATION SYSTEM

Adonis & Abbey Publishers Ltd

St James House
13 Kensington Square,
London, W8 5HD
United Kingdom

Website: http://www.adonis-abbey.com
E-mail Address: editor@adonis-abbey.com

Nigeria:
Suites C4 – C6 J-Plus Plaza
Asokoro, Abuja, Nigeria
Tel: +234 (0) 7058078841/08052035034

Copyright 2021 © Kgothatso B. Shai

British Library Cataloguing-in-Publication Data
A catalogue record for this book is available from the British Library

ISBN: 978-1-913976-00-2

The moral right of the author has been asserted

All rights reserved. No part of this book may be reproduced, stored in a retrieval system or transmitted at any time or by any means without the prior permission of the publisher

Scholarship and Politics in South Africa's Higher Education System

Kgothatso B. Shai

Dedication

*This book is dedicated:
firstly, to the late Onkgopotse Abram Tiro for standing for the truth against all odds;
secondly, to the University of Zululand's late Professor Gregory Kamwendo whose blood continues to nourish the tree of academic honesty in South Africa; and thirdly, to all youthful victims of academic bullying for staying true to their convictions.
With revolutionary love!*

An outstanding work of bravery and courage amid vast prevalence of academic bullying in South Africa. In this book, Professor Shai grabs the bull by its horn, tackling predominantly un-professorial tendencies of some of the old guards whose intellectual prowess seem to have reached a point of calamity. Youthful as he is, Shai unapologetically present a methodical critique of complexities surrounding scholarship and publishing in Africa and South Africa in particular. In this book, Shai has asserted himself as an epitome of Young people in scholarship, past "Afrocentricity" (His mantle), to deal with intricacies surrounding philosophical (multigenerational) contentions in academia.

Dr Thanyani Madzivhandila, School of Development Studies, University of Mpumalanga, Mbombela, South Africa.

The politics of scholarship in Africa is an important area that deserves the necessary attention of academics and all other interested stakeholders. However, the attention given to it has not been sufficient particularly focusing in South Africa. This book offers the necessary interest and appetite for other scholars to delve more into the subject of politics of scholarship.

Dr PH Munzhedzi, School of Management Sciences, University of Venda, Thohoyandou, South Africa.

Table of Contents

Contents iii
Dedication iv
Endorsement v
Preface viii

Part One
Discourses on Higher Education, Scholarship and Ethics

Chapter One
The death of scientific knowledge in [South] Africa: An Afrocentric response to MP Sebola 15

Chapter Two
[Un]masking Sebola's Mythology on the Politics of Scholarship in South Africa: An Afrocentric Youth Perspective 33

Chapter Three
Mokoko Sebola on 'Scientific Knowledge in Africa': An Afrocentric Critique. 49

Chapter Four
An Afrocentric Exploration of the nexus between Sebola'spolitricks of scholarship and [South] Africa's politics of the Doctoral Project 63

Chapter Five
Decay of scientific knowledge industry in Africa: An Afrocentric pre-parting shot 83

Chapter Six
Politicisation of university administration and implications for knowledge development in South Africa: An Afrocentric prognosis 99

Chapter Seven
Tawanda Nyawasha on Changing Scholarship in South Africa: An Afrocentric critique 113

Part two

Student Youth: the catalysts of social transformation

Chapter Eight
The Decriminalisation of the #FeesMustFall Movement in South Africa 127

Chapter Nine
Examining the Deficit of Youth Leadership in South Africa: An Afrocentric Student Perspective 147

Preface

The subject of the politics of scholarship (also read as scholarship of scholarship) in Africa is a hotbed between academics, observers, politicians, administrators, and students, among others. As it is the case in other parts of the world, the theory and practice of scholarly politics in Africa has proven to be complex and mainly misunderstood; the combined recipe that warrants a serious scholarly focus and attention. Because these politics are normally acted upon in a higher education terrain where the stakes are higher, the past of the state of scholarly politics in Africa is not uniformly understood at both the continental and global stage. Of late, Mokoko Sebola, Tawanda Nyawasha, and Molefi Asante have joined the bandwagon by raising controversial issues pertinent to scholarship in Africa. In this regard, their collective contributions which appear in different journals have reignited the interest in this subject and the pressing need for it to be deepened by volunteering complementary and/or counter-narratives. It is envisaged that our scholarship can only be bettered when there is open contestation of ideas or constructive intellectual warfare. Contextually, Sebola, and Nyawasha address different dimensions of scholarship in Africa. As it shall be seen, Sebola's thesis about the so-called death of knowledge was summarily and brutally killed by KgothatsoShai. On the other hand, Nyawasha's argument about the so-called "polemics of scholarship in South Africa" was exterminated by Asante. In the absence of any signs to stand and defend their ideas, one can only hope that Sebola and Nyawasha would find time to tender a public apology for advancing poorly thought out arguments about scholarship in Africa. Besides, Sebola and Nyawasha's contributions to this discourse reflect an ambitious task of hurriedly and briefly tackling a complex subject in a limited scope. The end product is bound to be "disappointment". As such, this book is an attempt to systematically and consistently bring to date the undiluted recollections of a leading Black South African academic about the practical realities of the politics of scholarship in Africa. These recollections are captured in the seven chapters which appear in part one of this book as an integrated critique against largely Sebola and to a particular extent; Nyawasha's Eurocentric intellectual onslaught. These are then completed with a further two chapters in part two of this book; which primarily deals with issues of students/youth activism in the higher education sector in South Africa. By and large, the earlier versions of some of these chapters were initially published as journal articles in the *Journal of Public Affairs* & *Commonwealth Youth and Development*, among others. To this end, we are greatly indebted to these journals for granting us the rare opportunity to test the viability of the raw ideas that germinated into this book product. These journals' permission for us to re-publish an improved and updated version of some of the chapters in this book is also highly appreciated. However, this book in its totality remains the author's original work.

It is noted that this subject remains under-researched and previous works in this regard were framed from a North[en] angled perspective. Hopefully, this book will serve as a stepping stone for future studies on this subject; especially for the Africans, Africa, and the international community. It is also painstaking that while this subject has been fairly debated among the Caucasians in Africa and beyond, there has been little effort by the Africans (Black South Africans in particular) to make a meaningful contribution towards this discourse. While Sebola and Nyawasha's contributions have served their purpose of keeping us on our toes in dialogue, I have fundamental political and theoretical differences with them. My well-considered view is that a fictitious reconciliation is not even necessary at this level. It is for this reason and the sake of the future of Africa that I compiled this book intending to reach a wider readership; which is willing to "un-think in order to re-think" properly to advance the shared agenda of Africans and anybody whose fate is tied to Africa.

What makes this book even more unique is that its author belongs to a completely different generation of scholars and intellectual tradition as compared to those who previously contributed to the extant body of knowledge on this subject. Yet he is a self-confessed Pan-Africanist. The author (a revered Afrocentric soldier of our generation) of this book is the product of the Afrocentric school, which is a re-enforcer of the innovative disruptive pedagogy. His thinking is largely influenced by Asante, a prominent African-American scholar who is broadly considered as the father of Afrocentricity. In appreciation of the need to defend the African archive in conversations about the politics of scholarship in Africa, the author of this book draws from Asante to dialogue with his supposed interlocutors (Sebola and Nyawasha). The approach followed in the writing of this book has proven to be good in that each of the chapters pursues different themes. However, there is an unavoidable element of duplication of a few arguments in different chapters. This is because they all seek to independently and in an integrated fashion, unmute the Afrocentric voice while largely critiquing the works of different authors to offer an alternative perspective about scholarship and politics in South Africa's higher education system. What follows now are the summaries of each chapter in the book.

Chapter 1: This chapter uses South Africa as a test case to critique Mokoko Piet Sebola's piece titled "Peer review, scholarship, and editors of scientific publications: the death of scientific knowledge in Africa", which appeared in *KOERS- Bulletin for Christian Scholarship*, Volume 83 (1): 1-13. I argue that Sebola's piece provides a partial guide to understanding the state of the knowledge industry in Africa, particularly in South Africa. Safe to say that Sebola's work deepens scholarly and public discourse on the politics of scholarship in Africa and the world at large. However, I do not intend to blatantly praise Sebola's contribution to this academic area, which remains under-researched due to the reasons that are beyond the scope of this chapter. In particular, this chapter aspires to identify scholarly weaknesses in Sebola's work to correct them by offering an alternative view. This correction deserves the attention of all scholars and practitioners especially because it is interdisciplinary and it is poised to undo the misinformation disseminated in Sebola's piece. Such misinformation has the potential to overshadow the few truths advanced in his article.

Chapter 2: This interdisciplinary review chapter extends the series of replies to Mokoko Piet Sebola's article referred to above. The aim of this chapter is two-fold: (i) to expose in detail the half-truths that have been overlooked in chapter 1st of this book due to sectional space constraints; (ii) To employ the theory of Afrocentricity for dis-abusing the hidden truths about scholarship from Sebola's nebulous editorial mythology. This chapter argues that the possibility of Sebola's unfortunate but systemic and consistent view on scientific knowledge in Africa (particularly in South Africa) being shared in oral or written form by his disciples cannot be ruled out. Given the inter-generational nature of this discourse, it is important that a corrective infusion based on the lived experience of intellectual African youth be proffered as a matter of urgency.

Chapter 3: This chapter extends a preliminary anti-thesis to Mokoko Piet Sebola's thesis alluded to above. Based on his piece, it is clear that the subject of the politics of scholarship is complex and not uniformly understood. In this chapter, I aim to critique Sebola's piece from an alternative Afrocentric perspective; a voice that has been emphatically marginalised in this academic discourse and beyond. In particular, I consistently and systematically refute his outlandish claim that scholarly editors and their peer review processes and mechanisms are responsible for the death of scientific knowledge in Africa. The importance of this interdisciplinary debate and the need for it to be expanded and/or sustained cannot be over-emphasised.

Chapter 4: In this chapter which uses the Doctoral Project in South Africa as a test case, I employ Afrocentricity as a theoretical and contextual lens to tease out deficient scholarly assertions in Sebola's article (referred to above), which constitute fundamental contradictions inherent in South Africa's academic landscape. In this regard, the central objective of this chapter is to explore the relationship between Sebola's *politricks* of scholarship and [South] Africa's politics of the Doctoral Project. At the centre of the thesis of this chapter, I argue that while Sebola's article is valuable to a limited extent, it masks his contribution (directly, complicitly, individually and collectively) to the quasi-death of serious scientific knowledge in Africa, particularly in South Africa.

Chapter 5: This chapter presents a pre-parting shot to a very interesting interdisciplinary debate that was started by Sebola and then, canonised by Shai. Sebola sought to argue that editors and their peer review process are a reason for the self-styled death of new scholarly knowledge. This argument was strongly challenged by Shai in a series of articles. Unfortunately, his supposed interlocutor went into proverbial hiding. He later re-engineered his nebulous argument in alternative elitist platforms wherein his 'word is treated as that of royalty, that deserves to be encircled with a kraal' as per African adage. There is no gainsaying that Sebola's work is more Eurocentric to reflect positively on African scholarship. I add to this debate by engaging Afrocentricity not just as a defence against Sebola's Eurocentric approach to the matter, but as an important view that can be used to promote African scholarship which remains understudied. I draw from a blend of critical discourse analysis and my lived experience as a young African academic in South Africa to reflect on the different parameters of scientific knowledge that Sebola could have explored but possibly left out due to a fixated narrative.[1]

Chapter 6: This chapter represents a parting shot to the heated subject of the politics of knowledge, which is not uniformly understood by both scholars and practitioners. It argues that much work in this regard is based on Northern angled perspectives; which are deficient in abilities to capture the essence of African reality. Based on qualitative materials and interdisciplinary discourse analysis, this chapter's primary focus is on the politicisation of university administration in South Africa. Taking a cue from my previous works on this subject, I have identified and discussed the additional three central factors which impair scientific knowledge generation and development in South Africa and Africa as a whole. Among others, these factors include bureaucratisation of academic administration, academic jealousy, and *gangsterism,* and shortage of academic role models. Theoretically and to foster epistemic justice, I have persistently drawn from Afrocentricity as an alternative contextual lens to paint a qualitatively rich picture of the phenomena under study.

Chapter 7: Unlike the Sebola/ Shai debate, Asante/ Nyawasha debate is a rich fortune for the scholarly community. In this chapter, I wish to synthesise the debate between Asante and Nyawasha. In particular, I aim to identify and address gross substantive scholarly weaknesses in Nyawasha's paper. I must hasten to re-state that I am proudly of Asante. I am greatly inspired and motivated to walk in the paths of the unsung Afrocentric de-colonial giants who came before us. My argument is that Nyawasha's paper is reflective of the lack of confidence in the thought system and knowledge that has sustained our forebears over many centuries. His paper is also a confirmation of the terrible hangovers of the colonial mental capture of the particular segment of the Black professoriate.

---

[1] This chapter and all others in this book are not necessarily a representation of my personal [his]story as an academic. But it is more of a scholarly recollection and reflection of the silenced voices. Therefore, this work should be broadly and unapologetically seen as an expression of the silenced and marginalised voices in the higher education sector in South Africa. Some of the silenced voices have confided to me and it is on this basis that they are referred in the certain instances as character X, Y and Z.

Chapter 8: During the struggle against colonialism and apartheid in South Africa and Africa, the liberation pioneers promised all citizens to access to decent education. The premise was that the education the colonial authorities made available to Africans was poor compared to that of white people. What was more, only some middle-class Africans were given access to higher education. The initiation of the protest movement #FeesMustFall in 2015 seemed to mark a crossroads in South Africa in terms of opening the doors of learning to all. However, some scholars and politicians argue that the country's higher education sector is still untransformed and inaccessible to most people. Still, others argue that the #FeesMustFall movement's call for an aggressive transformation of higher education has been hijacked by a "third force" to undermine the Government. In this chapter, I critique the competing perspectives of the ongoing public discourse on the #FeesMustFall movement based on interdisciplinary critical discourse and Afrocentric theory to gain a nuanced but critical understanding of this movement and its implications for the future. Notwithstanding the reservations about some of the bad elements of the modus operandi of the fallist movement, our major finding, as reported on in this chapter, was that the demand for quality and free higher education in South Africa was reasonable. Nevertheless, a decision to meet this demand might not be economically sound in respect to the immediate future.

Chapter 9: This chapter seeks to present and examine the part played by student movements in ensuring that youths are included as potential candidates in the electoral lists of democratic South Africa's political parties. The youths constitute the highest number of potential voters in South Africa's polls. There is enough evidence that demonstrates that the activism and energy of the youth are largely sought by political parties during electoral campaigns. Despite this, the representation of youths as candidates for South Africa's political parties is below expectations; except for the Economic Freedom Fighters (EFF). The poor representation of youths as candidates in the majority of South Africa's political parties raises questions in terms of their (political parties) commitment to youth development. As such, this chapter is an attempt to find answers for the following two central research questions: (1) To what extent do the students influence party politics? (2) Are the students active citizens? The author interrogates these questions using an

Afrocentric research methodology, which reinforces the dominant qualitative paradigm. This chapter concludes that most student movements in South Africa are used to fight factional battles and in the process; do very little to push for the inclusion of youth candidates during the elections.

Now that all is said and done, it is worth recording that this book will not have been successful without the generous support of the National Institute of Humanities and Social Sciences (NIHSS). Through the South African Association of Political Studies- Limpopo Chapter (SAAPS-LC), NIHSS has given me a scholarly lifeline by providing seed funding to advance political scholarship. This seed funding has successfully become an endowment that continues to benefit scholarly initiatives and projects of this nature in Limpopo Province and beyond. Lastly, I wish to thank God, my ancestors (the living dead) and family, students, comrades, friends, and colleagues in the South African Association of Public Administration and Management (SAAPAM), SAAPS, and other establishments in Africa and the diaspora for believing in my (the African child) abilities when I was at the brink of being withered away by the cauldron of academic storms and censorship by those who wield control of the corridors of power in Black universities. The struggle is our life! *Aluta Continua*!

CHAPTER ONE

The death of scientific knowledge in [South] Africa: An Afrocentric response to MP Sebola

Introduction

There is a paucity of academic literature on the politics of scholarship in South Africa (Chasi, 2015). This can be largely attributed to the fact that globally, and South Africa in particular, there are very few scholars (if there is any) that specialise in the politics of scholarship. Due to the multi-dimensional diversity and mosaic nature of Africa, by and large, I am using South Africa as a test case (Chazan, 1988). In this chapter, I also embrace the narrow meaning of politics as the struggle for power (Morgenthau, 1948). The limited academic literature which is available in this regard is mainly in the form of editorials. This is also complemented by scant academic literature produced by activist scholars such as Mokoko Piet Sebola, who is the author of the article under review. It is instructive for the reader to note that issues about the politics of scholarship are at times reflected in passing within journal articles that focus on certain topical societal issues (Phago, 2015). The foregoing observation should be understood within the context that the manifestations of the knowledge structure of the political economy have spillover effects on security, economic, trade, and financial structures of the political economy (Shai, 2017). Meanwhile, there is some official literature in the form of commissioned reports that evaluate South African Post-Secondary Education (SAPSE) accredited journals (Mouton, et al 2016). On the other hand, there is a build-up of popular literature (as featured in national newspapers) on the issues that are pertinent to the well-being of scholarship in South Africa (Motau, 2018). It is envisaged that the seriousness of the issues about the politics of scholarship as brought to the fore by mainstream media would stimulate the public and academic interest in this subject.

It is on this basis that Sebola's article is timely and relevant. This submission should not be mistaken to suggest that his contribution is breaking the ground on this subject. Other scholars have remarkably made seminal scholarly interventions in this regard; to a point of producing monographs such as the one published by the Africa Institute of South Africa (Ngobeni, 2010). The thrust of the engagement of this subject by Ngobeni (2010) and other like-minded scholars is fairly discussed in the subsequent sections of this chapter. It is thus commendable that Sebola has attempted to extend the frontiers of knowledge in this regard. Let me hasten to point out that the major weakness in Sebola's article is that facts have been clouded with misinterpretations, misperceptions, and to a certain extent, misunderstandings. Only time will tell as to whether the aforementioned misnomers are deliberate or rather driven by the desire to advance a particular selfish and narrow agenda. However, to fully understand the thrust of this chapter, it is important to put the reader into my confidence by hinting at a brief bio-sketch of Sebola.

Sebola is a well-known professor of Public Administration and Director of the School of Economics and Management at the University of Limpopo, in South Africa (University of Limpopo, 2018). He is also the editor of the privately owned and managed *Journal of Public Administration and Development Alternatives* (JPADA)- a by-product of his flagship project which is known as the International Conference on Public Administration and Development Alternatives (IPADA). *JPADA* is managed and owned by a "relatively unknown" commercial company called Batalea Publishers, whose sole director is none other than Sebola (Manyaka, 2016a). Equally important, it is worth noting that until May 2018 Sebola has served for several years as a member of the national board of the South African Association of Public Administration and Management (SAAPAM), the owner and oversight body for the prestigious *Journal of Public Administration* (JOPA) (Global Society of Scientific Research, 2019). To this effect, he also had an opportunity to serve as a guest editor of some of the special editions of *JOPA*, especially those derived from the proceedings of the Limpopo Chapter of SAAPAM. During his tenure as a member of the national board of SAAPAM, he also served as the chairperson of its Limpopo Chapter. While I welcome Sebola's contribution to this subject, obviously with reservations, I am frightened by his audacity to enter into the discourse of judgement. Outside of Limpopo, his academic credentials at the continental and global level do not put him in a safe space to enter into a discourse of this nature. Ordinarily, the discourse of judgement is the province of scholars who are at the cutting edge of research in their disciplines as confirmed by their peers (Sithole, 2009).

Towards an Afrocentric methodological and theoretical framing

This chapter is located within the realm of Afrocentric research methodology, which is broadly considered as a re-enforcer of the main qualitative research paradigm (Reviere, 2001; Shai, 2016). Even though this chapter was largely dependent on the discourse analysis of publications and a series of conversations with academics and research administrators of varying rankings and institutional affiliations in South Africa; it also immensely benefitted from my personal experience as an African scholar and analyst. Although often less acknowledged, dependence on the author's personal experience is not uncommon in qualitative studies, particularly those that are African-centred (Shai, 2017). It also carries spectacular currency in Afrocentric studies; because the latter's epistemic location compels them to reject the binary standing of knowledge as subjective or objective; empirical or non-empirical; good or evil. This premise should be understood within the context that naturally/ in an African context subjective and objective/ empirical and non-empirical bits of knowledge complement each other (Maserumule, 2011).

The foregoing observation dovetails with the Afrocentric conviction that epistemologies are the by-products of the value system of a particular society that practices them (Scheurich& Young 1997). Beyond the positivist dictates, my well-considered position is that the centrality of literature synthesis and personal experiences cannot be easily dismissed. Concerning this, it also goes without saying that if research is not personal, then the motivation is lost. Equally important, the positivists' envisaged empty perceptual space between the researcher and those researched is far-fetched, and therefore, its existence is overly dismissed in this chapter (Baugh &Guion, 2016). Contextually, the following three steps in discourse analysis as elucidated by Norman Fairclough (as cited by Horvath, 2014) were applied in the execution of the research for the current chapter: **D**escription focused on the formal properties of the text; **I**nterpretation centred on the nexus between text and interaction.

This entails the viewing of a text as an outcome of the production process and as a resource in interpretation, and Explanation examined the link between interaction and social context - with the social determination of the production and interpretation processes, and their social effects. The emerging discourse from the steps outlined above was complemented by an Afrocentric synthesis of the major findings through thematic analysis.

Meanwhile, the operationalisation of the research for this review chapter was underpinned by the theory of Afrocentricity as articulated by Asante (2003). The choice of this theory in this chapter was largely inspired by its cognitive and functional roles and/or abilities (Mazama, 2003). It also draws from the academic works of like-minded Afrocentric scholars such as Modupe (2003), Mazama (2003), and Carruthers (1999), just to mention a few. In this chapter, Afrocentricity is understood as a theory and paradigm which seeks to re-assert African agency in thought and practice within the livelihood of the Africans, their societal institutions, and processes (Shai, Molapo & Sodi, 2017). It is for this reason that Afrocentricity is introduced in this chapter as an alternative theoretical lens to dissect the state of scholarship in South Africa. This perspective immediately proffers a rupture from Sebola's work which is based on gatekeeping theory, which is speculative in nature and orientation. The utility value of gatekeeping theory in the analysis of the politics of scholarship in South Africa cannot be easily dismissed or rather, treated as if it does not exist. However, I argue that its careless use in unpacking issues relating to scholarship in Africa is extremely dangerous and has the potential to produce gross transversal or categorical trans-substantive errors as it is the case in Sebola's article (Azibo, 2011). The gatekeeping theory is rooted within the Euro-American worldview and its epistemological basis is the Euro-American value system, which is mainly driven by the notion of white supremacy in academy and all other aspects of life (Shai, 2017). It is unfortunate that in the article under review, the author (Sebola) fell for the trap of using borrowed epistemological lenses to try and understand the scholarly mechanisms and processes in Africa. As a result, his article wrongly paints a situation of despair and hopelessness regarding the state of scientific knowledge on the continent. In this context, a cauldron of despair and hopelessness serves as a time bomb for intellectual disorientation, miseducation, and de-education (Carruthers, 1999).

The foregoing observation should be understood within the context that unlike propaganda, the idea behind the dissemination of knowledge through articles is to inform and educate (Mazama, 2003). Concerning the above, Sebola (2018: 2) notes that "… no alternative theory is acceptable by any journal since journals exists not to challenge any existing theory of their scope but to maintain and channel the knowledge direction determined by the editor whether old or new". This is an outlandish claim. It wrongly generalises the alleged/ known practices and mechanisations of one journal (or editor) to all. Extrapolation does not normally attract credibility and reliability within the scholarly circles and in the case of the article under review, it only produced a disappointing mirage.

Besides, it is acceptable for journals to assume and maintain either a subject-specific, interdisciplinary, multidisciplinary, or transdisciplinary posture. Such a pre-determined posture is not necessarily arrived through the unilateral decision of the editor, but it also has more do with the interests and aspirations of the readership. As such, any author needs to familiarise himself/ herself with the focus and readership of his/her targeted journal beforehand for the sake of ensuring that s/he does not later cry foul to peer review without any sound basis. Emerging from this, it is the well-considered view of the current chapter that the politics of scholarship in South Africa and Africa at large can best be understood when studied through the prism of African-centred values, standards, and tools such as Afrocentricity (Asante, 1990). At the heart of Afrocentricity is the urgent need for studies on African issues, mechanisms or processes like peer review, to be centred on African culture, history, and values. Among others, African value systems include interdependence, cooperation, selflessness, and communalism (Mazama, 2003).

I do not imply that Afrocentricity displaces the use of gatekeeping theory in dissecting this subject. My argument is that the Afrocentric perspective is one voice among many voices. As an integral part of inclusive epistemology, Afrocentricity is well-positioned to foster an epistemic justice in an emerging discipline of the politics of scholarship, which has been largely researched and reported through alien epistemological lenses (Nabudere, 2012). While gatekeeping theory helps us to gain a greater sense of the complex practices of the selection of journal articles for publication, the introduction of Afrocentricity in this discourse assists in providing a proper context in the interpretation and analysis of the heads of arguments in the current chapter. That knowledge is socially constructed also finds expression in social constructivism and quantum physics (Shai, 2017).

Scholarly peer review in [South] Africa: Reconsidered?

Regardless of its imperfections, the importance of scholarly peer review in the production and dissemination of scientific knowledge cannot be over-emphasised. There is an avalanche of scientific knowledge that echoes this sentiment (Sithole, 2009; Ngobeni, 2010; Muchie &Baskaran, 2013). Among other functions of peer review includes: ensuring that factually correct and scientifically credible knowledge is disseminated; guarding against the exchange of knowledge in articles that are otherwise polluted by substantive editorial errors and "gatekeeping" the publication of irrelevant or misguided information. Contrary to the claim that the article under review was peer-refereed, it would appear that all of the aforementioned weaknesses find real and honest expression in it (Sebola's work). For example, notes from reviewers were published immediately after the reference list, something which is quite strange in the journal circles. Africa is also mistakenly referred to as a country. While the notes that are purported to be coming from the reviewers are constructive, it is sad that they were not considered before publication and this makes their inclusion in the article very embarrassing. That in itself raises serious questions about *KOERS*' commitment to thorough peer review and the production of quality articles. It may not be too far-fetched to submit that the quality of the article under review and the credibility of its peer review raises fundamental questions relating to the "real existence" of the editorial board in *KOERS*. If it indeed exists beyond mere naming; it may be time for its job description and relationship with the editor to be revisited or at most, professionalised especially within the broader context of author-editor relations.

Beyond this, the publication of the ill-prepared article by Sebola equally raises serious questions about the commitment of his own Batalea Publishers or *JPADA* to what he terms "ethical peer review" and to a larger extent, the production of quality articles. An attempt to find answers for fundamental questions relating to the above can only raise more questions, some of whose answers are provided hereunder. Elsewhere in the article, Sebola (2018:5) weakens his earlier insinuation about the bias of editors when he stresses that "[I]t's very difficult to determine the impartiality in the editors' selection of material for publication in the journal". It is equally not easy to prove the speculations about the bias of editors in deciding or not deciding to publish a particular manuscript (Sithole, 2009). It is therefore important that challenges concerning the good intentions of scholarly peer review are addressed in a multidimensional, rather than a linear fashion.

The foregoing analysis has one key lesson for Sebola and company that "if you live in a glasshouse, do not throw stones", as cautioned by the English adage. Apparently, peer review has meaningful benefits for the authors of articles, editors, journals, and their owners. Closer scrutiny of the article under review reflects serious reputational implications for its author, *KOERS*, its editorial board, and owners. Unless *KOERS* and other journals that operate in the same manner re-enforce their article peer review and production processes, they certainly run a risk of losing their SAPSE accreditation. It is critically important for all journals to "gate-keep" against tendencies that seek to abuse scientific platforms to hurl unwarranted insults and spit vitriol on thought-leading editors such as Mashupye H. Maserumule. In the same line of thinking, it cannot be correct that aggrieved scholars who currently or previously belonged to professional and scholarly associations such as SAAPAM can simply jump ship and stand on mountain tops for the sole purpose of exploiting their academic connectivity to undermine prestigious journals such as the *JOPA* and *AdministratioPublica* (Global Society of Scientific Research, 2019). Similarly, Ben Okri (as cited by Masoga, 2015) contends that mountain tops are meant for human beings to stand on them to gain a better view of the beauty of nature; not anything mischievous.

It is interesting to note that Sebola cries foul about *JOPA* and *Administratio Publica* on the question of page fees and other production-related matters in the same year that his own *JPADA* is due to apply for SAPSE accreditation. Since *JOPA* and *Administratio Publica* are the main leading journals in the discipline of Public Administration in South Africa, his timing for their criticism is questionable by any measurable standard. Strictly speaking, his wanton attacks on these journals can also be accounted for through the theory of anarchy as explained by Nabudere (2012). It is only in the intellectual world of the *Sebolas* that one emerging journal and its editor has to rubbish others to gain recognition. Sadly, such tendencies can be observed among African scholars; maybe they accidentally became Africans through their Black melanin. But in thinking and reality, they stand for white interests (Badat, 2009). This is because the tendencies that they espouse can only find expression in Euro-American value systems. Among others, Euro-American value systems include individualism, competition, and selfishness (Shai, 2016). I am making the foregoing observation with the full consciousness that I stand to be accused of ethnocentrism by the defenders of western civilisation (Carruthers, 1999). Even though this is my observation, it does not in any way constitute a racial slur but an abomination of a race-based system that seeks to entrench racially-motivated inequalities, discrimination, and related intolerances in the society. Regardless of the sensitivity of the latter, scholars need to debate it irrespective of whether it exists in reality or is just a perception. After all, this is what scholarship is all about; the contestation of ideas. The essence of problematisation of sensitive subjects in scholarship is well captured in Frank Chikane's (2013) book title "The Things that Could Not be Said".

Sebola (2018:3) avers that Maserumule's experience in the editorial chair of *JOPA* stood against his polemic editorial promise that "gatekeeping is the only solution to keep the integrity of scholarship of the *Journal of Public Administration*". This is a sweeping statement and the author hopelessly fails to keep us into confidence by providing proof for his damning, but baseless allegations against Maserumule. Maserumule's record insofar as his service to *JOPA* speaks for itself (Global Society of Scientific Research, 2019). During his tenure as the editor of *JOPA*, he successfully led collective efforts to change the layout of *JOPA* and against all odds, he progressively elevated *JOPA* to one of the top five South African journals in social sciences during the year 2016 (Mouton, 2016). This is a positive step that saw congratulatory messages coming from all corners of South Africa, especially the Department of Higher Education and Training (DHET) which does not shy away from taking pride in Black excellence as exhibited in *JOPA* editorship. Equally important, it is an undisputed fact that most of the articles appearing in *JOPA* have scholarly and policy implications. Concerning the latter, I am reminded of one article from *JOPA* that was cited in the ruling of the Electoral Court of South Africa. Conversely, the good work of *JOPA* and its editorial team can only be summed up through a Xitsonga expression: "mintirhoyavulavula"/ actions speak louder than words.

My impressions of SAAPAM is that its active membership and leadership may not necessarily reflect the realities of South Africa's population dynamics, but it is the undisputed truth that it remains a multiracial professional and scholarly formation of Public Administration in the country. Equally important, my encounter with *JOPA* a few years ago is symbolic of the breath of fresh air in terms of scholarly debates and democracy of thought (Maserumule, 2015a). Although a trained Political Scientist and relatively new to the discipline of Public Administration in South Africa, my often controversial intellectual infusions within this scholarly community were never rejected, supposedly because *JOPA* is one of the few journals in South Africa with a clear transformation agenda (Shai &Iroanya 2014; Maserumule, 2015b). *JOPA* tolerated and embraced my unconventional Afrocentric interventions to the development of the discipline of Public Administration in South Africa. This attitude is a total rupture from the one I have experienced with the author of the article under review, who openly, consistently, and unapologetically rejected Afrocentricity in content or through association; thereby arguing that it is nothing more than a representation of intellectual activism. Having said that, all credits for the positive attributes hinted above and others not mentioned here still goes to the editorial team under the leadership of Maserumule and KedibonePhago, who should not allow their thankless efforts to be distracted by horn-blowing professor(s) who understandably refuse to learn.

While I do not have anything personal against Sebola, my qualms with him and the larger segment of the ageing South African professoriate is the apparent unwillingness to read further and learn about a phenomenon before they criticise it (Maserumule, 2015b). Specifically, the foregoing analysis should be understood within the context that a few years ago, Sebola self-published a book entitled: *Local Government Administration in Post-Apartheid South Africa: Some Critical Perspectives*. This book was to be later reviewed by Rasodi K. Manyaka, who concluded that he was hesitant to recommend it for students based on gross weaknesses, including glaring editorials errors, poor conceptualisation of certain chapters, and unjustified deviation from some of the crucial conventions in the preparation of edited books, *inter alia*. Instead of Sebola drawing lessons from Manyaka's (2016) book review, he opted for selective reading to an extent that in his journal article under review, he proves that he remains a "full professor" who appears hesitant to learn from the young and upcoming scholars. Consequently, his writings are often polluted with gross editorial errors and factual inaccuracies which leave much to be desired (Sebola, 2017). It is against this backdrop that some scholars such as VusiGumede (2015) call for the urgent need for Africans emanating from different scholarly and ideological pursuits to engage in 'unlearning, relearning, unthinking and rethinking'.

Myths and realities in scientific editorship

Sebola (2018:4) posits that "[E]ditors are custodians of a research record achieved for solving political, economic and social problems in the society". While this observation dovetails with Maserumule's (2017) invocation of the "scholarship of consequences", Sebola's contention is partly true and it ought to be placed in a proper perspective to avoid deleterious misunderstandings. Thus some articles are simply aimed at enhancing the understanding of certain issues thereby extending literature and do not have obvious policy implications. Among the main functions of scientific editors, Sebola (2018:4) lists " ....constructive and immediate feedback to authors". It is worth noting that the supposedly constructive feedback that editors normally provide is solicited from the reviewers, with a few exceptions wherein the article was reviewed by the editor himself/herself. The latter is not unusual especially in the case of invited articles on critical special issues or in instances wherein the general turnaround in terms of the provision of reports by the assigned reviewers is poor (Molepo, 2019). My experience of being involved in convening the 2017 Limpopo/Gauteng Colloquium of the South African Association of Political Studies (SAAPS) in Polokwane and subsequent coordination of efforts to produce selected articles in some special journal editions has proven that in South Africa generally, there are very few well-established scholars who are willing to review papers and provide timeous feedback (Molepo, 2019). As such, Sebola's insinuation that scientific editors ought to provide immediate feedback is inconsiderate. His insinuation shows a lack of appreciation on his part that in the case of Africa, peer review and/or scientific editorship is a voluntary service by academics. It is a service that is rendered in the side-lines of the academics' full-time jobs.

Sebola (2018:5) laments that "[A]t the most a high number of reviewers rather recommend acceptance than rejection in publication". While this may be true, it also depends on the reviewer's area of expertise and academic training. Hence, an expert in a specialised subfield such as International Relations is likely to be familiar with existing arguments and currents debates relating to his/her research area as compared to a scholar who is ordinarily trained and grounded in either Tourism Studies, Educational Management or Theology. So it is important that specific articles be allocated to subject-specific experts, who are well-positioned to offer constructive and relevant expert review/advice as compared to a simple comprehension of generalities. A year ago a colleague of mine at the University of South Africa (Unisa) once confided to me that the higher rejection rate in a certain politics journal in South Africa is well planned and orchestrated to assist its editor to deal with a huge backlog of article submissions which were long over-due for processing. This privileged information settled my fears about my academic writing abilities, after two different articles I have penned were rejected in the journal in question. Despite this and as a young African scholar, I positively drew pointers from the comments on the rejected manuscripts for improvement and I later on submitted such to other scientific platforms where they received favourable reviews and ultimately got published (Smit, 2019). This section of the current chapter raises issues that speak to the practical realities of fundamental ethical issues within and between academic disciplines.

Among other benefits of impressive scientific publications record identified by Sebola (2018:5) is the improved "ranking of a university in the scholarship". While this is largely true, the overall global university ranking criteria of certain formations have been contested in certain quarters of Africa. Nevertheless, I add that the financial incentives derived from publication earnings by scholars in certain universities in South Africa largely explain the emerging tendency by some to persistently attack editors who reject their manuscripts, regardless of their publishability or non-publishability (Motau, 2018). It is on this basis that it is not uncommon in certain universities in South Africa to find professors who cannot profess knowledge. While such professors are generally boastful, a quick perusal of the citation index of their sole-authored articles reflects self-citation; which is evident that their work has limited or no impact as they are not read or consulted by their peers (Manyaka, 2016b).

Sebola (2018:5) believes that "[T]he editor has a moral responsibility to edit the idea to suit what the author wanted to convey to the scientific community". Considering that what is moral or ethical for one segment of the population may not be the same for the other, I would prefer to say that it is the editors' humanitarian responsibility to lend a helping hand to those in need of such and are willing to receive it. This is normally a daunting and challenging editorial task when it comes to established scholars who are not fully conscious of their writing weaknesses [unconscious incompetence] or simply refusing to learn at an older age [conscious incompetence]. Nonetheless, it could be argued that Sebola and the editorial leadership of *KOERS* have a shared humanitarian and professional responsibility to ensure that all sources cited in the former's article (under review) are included in the reference list. This is a responsibility that they deliberately and collectively failed to execute in respect of Maserumule and NghamulaNkuna. Could the exclusion of these authors' works from the reference list be attributed to their differences of opinion with the author? Alternatively, are they intentionally omitted because the author does not want to raise or elevate their citation profile and journal index? Whatever the case, it is extremely unethical and the complicity of *KOERS* editorial leadership in this regard is worrisome.

In the article under review, Sebola (2018: 5-6) unconsciously self-inflicts reputational injuries when he addresses that "… self-publication by the author may reveal a shocking compromise of a peer review process by the chief editor himself". I argue that Sebola does not have moral *locus standi* to raise this genuine concern, which obviously cannot be overlooked in instances of clear abuse of editorial powers. This is because more often than not and as/ whenever Sebola secures a publication space in a form of a special edition in a SAPSE accredited journal and when he then serves as a guest editor [i.e. *African Journal of Public Affairs*, Vol 9 (5)], his name tends to appear in no less than two articles (see the year 2012 *JOPA* special edition, Vol 1, 47). This cannot be wholly symptomatic of intellectual prowess on his part. Perhaps, it shows the extent to which research incentives derived from publication earnings provide a fertile ground for the germination of seeds for unethical practices in respect of co-authorship. To add, his guest-editorship for special editions of accredited journals or edited books largely benefited his confidantes at the expense of scholarly excellence by non-close associates. The essence of the foregoing analysis can be found in the Sotho expression "*Se bone selabileihlong la ngwaneno o palelwakekwata go la gago*". Essence to it can also be borrowed from the biblical book John 8: 1-11. The rough meaning of the aforementioned Sotho figurative expression and biblical scripture denotes that the things we blame others for doing are the same things we are to be later found to be doing.

Conclusion

Based on the critical review and Afrocentric analysis advanced above, it can be concluded that the study of the politics of scholarship in South Africa can best be understood when located within the broader African and historical context. In the contemporary world, it cannot be true for some "holy cows" to exploit Woodrow Wilson's seminal article in *Political Science Quarterly* as the excuse for submitting half-baked manuscripts for publication consideration in scientific journals. Even if it is true that the then editor of *Political Science Quarterly* overlooked structure and academic rigour in favour of novelty in deciding on Wilson's article; it is argued that times have changed now and every publication outlet has its rules and regulations which must be observed by any potential author. An easier route for failing to conform to such established guidelines can be self-publishing, and Sebola is already making inroads in this regard.

This unpopular practice of being a "player and referee" does not cast Sebola as a paragon of high ethical principles and standards in scholarship. Hence, the edited book(s) that he self-publishes are also sold to most of the contributing authors of individual chapters and yet, they never receive royalties for their intellectual properties. Surely, a common practice for the publishing industry shows that contributing authors to edited books are eligible for complimentary copies, even if it means one copy and subsequently, discounted prices on the book where their intellectual productions feature. But the same cannot be said about Sebola's Batalea Publishers. As the English adage has it that "charity begins at home", perhaps it is timely for Sebola and company to seriously inculcate ethical values in their backyard before they could unleash unwarranted attacks against sober, selfless, progressive, and competent peer reviewers and editors of scientific publications.

Unlike the article under review, it is my humble submission that serious scholarship goes beyond the collection of allegations, emotional undertones, pro/ self-incrimination, and aggrieved posturing. In the final analysis, the article under review falls below the bar for serious scholarship. But it is hoped that it will reignite policy and scholarly interest in the politics of scholarship in South Africa. Last but not least, the research for the current study has found that the gate-keeping theory only provides a partial guide to the understanding of the discourse on the politics of scholarship in South Africa. Its utility value stands to be enhanced when it is supplemented with other context-sensitive and alternative theoretical perspectives such as Afrocentricity and decoloniality (Nkuna&Shai 2018).

References

Asante M.K. 1990.*Kemet, Afrocentricity and Knowledge*. Trenton: Africa World Press.

Asante M.K. 2003.Afrocentricity: *The Theory of Social Change*. Chicago: African American Images.

Azibo D.A. 2011. Understanding Essentialism as Fundamental: The Centred African Perspective on the Nature of Prototypical Human Nature- Cosmological Ka (Spirit).*The Western Journal of Black Studies*, Vol 35 (2): 77-91.

Badat S. 2009. *Black Man, you are on your own*. Braamfontein: Steve Biko Foundation.

Baugh E.J. &Guion L. 2016.Using culturally sensitive methodologies when researching diverse cultures.*Journal of MultiDisciplinary Evaluation*, 4:1-12.

Bible (n.d.), New Jerusalem Version (NJV). John 8: 1-11.

Carruthers J.H. 1999. *Intellectual Warfare*. Chicago: Third World Press.

Chasi C.T. 2015. How to speak of Speak of Ending Apartheid Humanities: Transformation, Renaissance, Metamorphosis or Resurrection? *Journal of Public Administration*, Vol 50 (2): 174-190.

Chazan N. 1988.*Politics and Society in Contemporary Africa*. Basingstoke: Macmillan.

Chikane F. 2013. *The Things that Could Not be Said*. Johannesburg: Picador Africa

Global Society of Scientific Research.(2019, January).Letter from Journal Impact Factor Team to the Editorial Board of the *Journal of Public Administration*.

Gumede V. 2015.Exploring the Role of Thought Leadership, Thought Liberation and Critical Consciousness for Africa's Development.*Africa Development*, Vol XI (4): 91-111.

Horvath, J. 2014. *Critical Discourse Analysis of Obama's Political Discourse*. http://www.pulib.sk/elpub2/FF/Ferencik2/pdf_doc/6.pdf (Accessed 02 September 2014).

Klenert S. & Wager E. 2010. Responsible research publication: international standards for editor. A position statement developed at the 2nd world conference on research integrity in a global environment. Imperial College Press/ World Scientific Publishing, Singapore: 3-28.

Manyaka R.K. &Sebola M.P. 2012.Impact of performance management on service delivery in the South African public service.*Journal of Public Administration*, Vol 47 (Special issue 1): 299-310.

Manyaka R.K. 2016a. Book Review- Local Government Administration in Post-Apartheid South Africa: Some Critical Perspectives, MP Sebola (Ed.). *Journal of Public Administration*, Vol 51 (3): 436-441.

Manyaka, R.K. (2016b, October 18) RE: Supervision. An email message from a former academic employee of the University of Limpopo to Prof MP Sebola (main supervisor/ Director of the School of Economics and Management, University of Limpopo).

Maserumule, M.H. 2011. Good Governance in the New Partnership for Africa's Development (NEPAD: A Public Administration Perspective. Unpublished PhD Thesis. Pretoria: University of South Africa.

Maserumule M.H. 2015a. Ecdysis of Inhibition.*Journal of Public Administration*, Vol 50 (2): 172-173.

Maserumule M.H. 2015b. Engaged Scholarship and Liberatory Science: A Professoriate, Mount Grace, and SAAPAM in the Decoloniality Mix. *Journal of Public Administration*, Vol 50 (2): 200-222.

Maserumule M.H. 2017.*Journal of Public Administration* matters, a presentation at the conference of the South African Association of Public Administration and Management (SAAPAM), May 2017, Empangeni (Kwazulu Natal), Umfolozi Hotel.

Masoga E. 2015. "Keynote Address", presented at the Independent Electoral Commission (IEC) Limpopo Provincial Youth Summit, Forever Resorts (Bela-Bela), 23-25 March 2015.

Mazama A. (Ed). 2003. *The Afrocentric Paradigm*. Trenton: Africa World Press.

Modupe D.S. 2003. The Afrocentric Philosophical Perspective: Narrative Outline. In Mazama A. (Ed).*The Afrocentric Paradigm*. Trenton: Africa World Press.

Molepo J. (2019, January 16). Re: Review Session. An email message from the Executive Director of SAAPAM National Board to selected reviewers for articles submitted for consideration in the *Journal of Public Administration*.

Morgenthau, HJ. 1948. *Politics Among Nations: The Struggle for Power and Peace*. New York: Alfred A. Knopf.

Motau K. 2018. SAAPAM Chief Editor 'threatened' after rejection of some articles. *Eyewitness News* (online), https://ewn.co.za/2018/03/03/saapam-chief-editor-threatened-after-rejection-of-some-articles (Accessed 03 March 2018).

Motubatse K.N, Ngwakwe C.C. &Sebola M.P. 2017. The effect of governance on clean audits in South African municipalities.*African Journal of Public Affairs*,Vol 9 (5): 90-102.

Mouton J; Valentine A. & Spies J. 2016.An analysis of SA journals. PowerPoint presentation delivered during the National Editors Forum meeting, ASSAf, 1 September 2016.

Muchie M. &Baskaran A. (Eds) 2013.*Building Innovation in Africa: Case Studies*. Pretoria: Africa Institute of South Africa.

Nabudere D.W. 2012.*Afrikology and Transdisciplinarity: A Restorative Epistemology*. Pretoria: Africa Institute of South Africa.

Ngobeni S. (Ed) 2010. *Scholarly Publishing in Africa: Opportunities and Impediments*. Pretoria: Africa Institute of South Africa.

Nkuna N.W. &Sebola M.P. 2012. Public administration theoretical discourse in South Africa and the developmental local government: A need to go beyond modern thinking. *Journal of Public Administration*, Vol 47 (Special issue 1): 68-87.

Nkuna V.M. &Shai K.B. 2018.An exploration of the 2016 violent protests in Vuwani, Limpopo province of South Africa.*Man in India*, Vol 98 (3): 425-436.

Phago K.G. 2015. Transmogrifying Public Administration Scholarship and Praxis in South Africa.*Journal of Public Administration*, Vol 50 (2): 223-233.

Reviere R. 2001. Toward an Afrocentric research methodology. *Journal of Black Studies*, Vol 31 (6): 709-728.

Sebola M.P. 2012. Objective role of the South African media industry: The watchdogs for good governance and service delivery. *Journal of Public Administration*, Vol 47 (Special issue 1): 407-419.

Sebola M.P. & Tsheola J.P. 2017. Complexities of governance formality and informality for developing countries: Editorial perspective. *African Journal of Public Affairs*,Vol 9 (5): 1-7.

Sebola M.P. 2017. Governance of South Africa's Higher Learning Institutions: Complexities of internal stakeholder engagement in universities. *African Journal of Public Affairs*,Vol 9 (5): 179-189.

Sebola M.P. Ed. 2017.*Local Government Elections, Politics & Administration*.Polokwane: Batalea Publishers.

Sebola M.P. 2018. Peer review, scholarship and editors of scientific publications: the death of scientific knowledge in Africa. *KOERS-Bulletin for Christian Scholarship*, Vol 83 (1):1-13.

Shai K.B. 2016. An Afrocentric Critique of the United States of America's foreign policy towards Africa: The case studies of Ghana and Tanzania, 1990-2014. Unpublished Ph.D. Thesis.Sovenga: University of Limpopo.

Shai K.B. 2017. South African State Capture: A Symbiotic Affair between Business and State Going Bad (?). *Insight on Africa*, Vol 9 (1): 1-14.

Shai K.B, Molapo R.R. &Sodi T. 2017. The United States of America's post-1990 foreign policy towards West Africa: The case study of Ghana. *Journal for Contemporary History*, Vol 42 (1): 154-173.

Shai K.B. &Iroanya R.O. 2014.A critical appraisal of the American ideological position on Africa's democritisation.*Journal of Public Administration*, Vol 49 (3): 909-923.

Scheurich, J.J. & Young, M.D. 1997.Coloring epistemologies: Are our research epistemologies racially biased? *Educational Researcher*, 26(4):4-16.

Sithole M.P. 2009.*Unequal Peers*. Pretoria: Africa Institute of South Africa.

Smit J.A. 2019. RE: Your Article: Interface Between Constitutional Democracy and Traditional Mechanisms of Authority in Rural

Communities of South Africa: Lessons from Maruleng. An email message from the Chief Editor of *Alternation* journal to an author.

University of Limpopo. 2018. School of Economics and Management Acting Director: Professor Mokoko Sebola.http s://www.ul.ac.za/index.php?Entity=School%20Main%20Menu&school_id=5 (Accessed 20 November 2018).

CHAPTER TWO

[Un]masking *Sebola*'s Mythology on the Politics of Scholarship in South Africa: An Afrocentric Youth Perspective

Introduction

The subject on the politics of scholarship in South Africa, Africa and the developing world remains under-researched (Shai, 2019). While no single factor can be solely attributed to this, it is safe to state that generally, there are very few (if there is any) academics who specialise on this subject. The foregoing observation should be understood within the context that the politics of scholarship is not a stand-alone academic discipline within the conventional mix in knowledge faculties, which is by by-product of North[ern] angled thought system (Ndlovu-Gatsheni, 2018). As such, there is no clear picture about the state of scholarship in South Africa. To a limited extend, lack or scarcity of targeted funding on this subject cannot be ruled out among those main factors that cause the poverty of knowledge on scholarship in South Africa and elsewhere (Shai, 2017; Macupe, 2019). It is for this reason that this phenomenon has become a soft target for misperception, misinterpretations and misunderstanding. The paucity of literature on the politics of scholarship in South Africa cannot also be wholly delinked from the general low research outputs by Africans and from Africa. Contextually, the limited literature on the politics of scholarship has been largely produced by activist scholars from the conventional academic disciplines such as Political Science, Public Administration and Law, *inter alia*; most of whom are old (Maserumule, 2015a; Maserumule, 2015b). The foregoing observation suggests that there is limited time, energy and resources that are invested in the study of the politics of scholarship. Regardless of this, what clearly emerges from the limited literature on this subject is that it is polarised in terms of the value (or lack) of peer review and scientific editorship. It is for this reason that this article attempts to [un]mask the mythology on the politics of scholarship as articulated by MP Sebola. For the purpose of this chapter, mythology is understood as an umbrella term which denotes a systematic and consistent set of ideas that are based on claims that are either not real, or are false.

While Sebola's narrative cannot be rejected at face value, it is important to point out that whether it is deemed as a reality or myth, it is socially constructed (Baylis, Smith & Owens, 2008; Shai, 2016). It is just one voice among many complementary or competing voices (Azibo, 2011). It is for this reason that this chapter attempts to sift earlier overlooked lies in Sebola's article by offering alternative truths based on the experiences of the African youth. This aim or rather proposition is inspired by the slain Guinean revolutionary, Amilcar Cabral who asserted that "Hide nothing from the masses of our people. Tell no lies. Expose lies whenever they are told. Mask no difficulties, mistakes, failures. Claim no easy victory". Perhaps for the purpose of context it should be pointed out that this chapter is not a personal attack on Sebola. However, its epistemic (Afrocentric) location forces it to assume a position that rejects the perceptual space between the researcher/ author and his views/ findings (Milam, 1992). This is because the researcher occupies a central position in the conceptualisation and operationalisation of research. While Sebola's version of the subject of this chapter may be accepted in certain circles, the truth is that there are always two sides of the story (Asante, 2003).

According to Sebola (2018:1) "the manner in which the scholarship peer review as process of scientific quality is conducted and perceived in the editorial arena is a cause of insufficient knowledge production in Africa". Before delving into the merits of this argument, it is worth-noting beforehand that it is ill-defined and is evident of the danger of assuming a simplistic approach in dealing with complex problems or situations. The "manner" implied in Sebola's invocation as cited above cannot be wholly responsible for the disappointing pace of scientific knowledge production by the Africans. Besides, it is better to produce insufficient scientific knowledge which is globally competitive, but locally relevant (i.e. policy-relevant knowledge) with both scholarly and policy implications (Shai, Molapo & Sodi, 2017). Regardless of this, the claim that Africa is producing less than 2% of academic literature is debatable and even if it is true, its advocates often fail to provide a proper context for it. Considering the colonial history of the major part of Africa, it is unfathomable for any scholar to compare her (Africa) with other continents without a colonial history (Boahen, 2003). The sad thing about this form of intellectual bankruptcy is the tendency to use foreign standards and tools (i.e. gatekeeping theory) to evaluate Africa's knowledge industry and developmental path. Instead of settling for the easier inward looking into Africa, this research therefore argues that any reference to Africans must be explicit and entail those of the land, blood or both (Hussein, 1998). The foregoing observation should be understood within the context that Africans born and residing outside the continent have a cultural citizenship to Africa (Carruthers, 1999). As such, Africa has a legitimate right to claim their achievements in the knowledge industry and other areas of life. This conceptualisation and contextualisation of Africans renders Sebola's argument in this regard as nothing more than an "uneducated guess" hidden in the veil of professorship.

Methodological and theoretical contours

The aim of this chapter is largely achieved through document study and interdisciplinary critical discourse analysis in its broadest form. Equally important, the hinging of this chapter on the theory of Afrocentricity directs it to also tap into the past experiences and encounters with the editors of a variety of journals in South Africa and beyond. This knowledge was complemented by my informal conversations with research managers of different institutions in South Africa, research administrators and assistants, emerging and well-established scholars. In an underlying quest of this chapter to promote African interests in academy and other aspects of life in the international system, the chapter has also drawn from the culture, history and motifs of the Africans (Asante, 2003). What is predominantly purported as objectivity by traditional social scientists is accepted in this chapter as the collective subjectivity of the Europeans and Americans (Reviere, 2001). Emerging from this premise and in order to enhance the adequacy of the functional role of this Afrocentric chapter (Mazama, 2003), I (young scholar) have occupied a central position during the operationalisation of its research in relation to qualitative data materials with a view to exposing and defeating all forms of intellectual dictatorship often displayed by some of the old academics (Sebola, 2018). However, the colossal shaping of this chapter's research process by me was not done at the expense of the actual reflections of those who were generous to casually share their experiences in so far as the politics of scholarship in South Africa is concerned. This submission does not imply that interviews were conducted for this work, which remains a review chapter that has immensely benefited from my intellectual resources which were shaped by previous encounters with those who have been at the coalface of the practice of this subject.

The state of research publications in Africa: Revisited?

Joseph Goebbels once echoed that "repeat a lie often enough and it becomes the truth" (as cited by Stafford, 2016). But my mother disagrees when she argues that "you cannot bury the truth in the sand because its strength will simply push it to re-surface". But the several academic and factual flaws on Sebola's article could be attributed to the fact that he has lied to himself several times about his intellectual sharpness to a point wherein he believed himself. Against the factual mishaps advanced in Sebola's article, the attention of the reader is drawn to the fact that Africa is a diverse and mosaic continent with 54 independent nation states characterised by uneven levels of socio-economic development (Chazan, 1988; Shai, 2016). The insensitive labelling of Africa as underdeveloped in the article under review vindicates my belief about its author's ignorance of the dynamics of economic geography in the continent. Whatever the precarious socio-economic condition that African states, individually and collectively, find themselves is not permanent. That developmental efforts are continuously conceived and experimented in Africa shows the continent's potential to liberate itself from poverty to victory in development (Asante, 2003; Shai, 2013). Such oscillating events can only give any serious scholar a sense of hope that Africa is indeed "developing". Unfortunately, Sebola uses a confused epistemological identity to try to paint a picture of the *politricks* (denotes the complexity of politics as a dirty business that involves an incalculable number of tricks) of scholarship in Africa, a misstep that could only result in further intellectual mis-orientation and mis-education and mis-location and dis-location (Carruthers, 1999).

While Africa may be lagging behind on global race in respect of the production of research publications; the point is that there is no convincing evidence to wholly blame this continent for such a setback in the knowledge structure of the global political economy (Shai, 2017).

Imperialism, colonialism and apartheid hang-overs have a bearing on the minimal contribution of Africans and Africa to the knowledge structure of the global political economy (Boahen, 2003; Shai, 2009; Lekane & Asuelime, 2017; Nkuna & Shai, 2018). It is my conviction that comparing African states individually or collectively with their North American or European counter parts is tantamount to a comparison of apples and oranges. Thus, the context for their evolution in respect of knowledge production varies and any attempt to properly understand such should be located within a proper context.

Scientific editors' control of knowledge production and dissemination

According to Sebola (2018:2) scientific editors "have same functions of sifting relevant and appropriate information fit for the purpose of the journal leaving others which do not seem to serve their purpose". This assertion contradicts the view advanced earlier by Sebola that editors publish articles for their own purpose, rather than that of the authors. This contention is also not well-thought of. It constitutes a generalisation which is certainly difficult to prove. There may be few instances wherein the existence of such practices can be tested. But such cannot be used to guarantee or paint a bleak picture of academic peer review and editorship in its entirety. Such contradiction vindicates my strong belief that as the author, journal editor and publisher in his own right, Sebola (2018:2) is surely battling with an internal and external conflict in terms on how best and honest can he discourse on the fundamental issues that cut across this subject. Sebola persists with his controversial tirade when he submits that journals "exist to sell a particular scientific perspective than the opposite perspective that can be pushed by authors of a different opinion". It is my well-considered view that this submission by Sebola is factually incorrect. It is also dangerous for Sebola to pass sweeping statements and generalisations without any empirical evidence. Whether this is real or not, the fact is that his failure to use case studies to illustrate his point risk real time irreparable reputational damage to scientific editorship and scholarship as a whole.

Sebola also makes an assumption that most authors are not comfortable in speaking out against unethical scientific editorship due to the fear for reprisals. These reprisals can be in the form of "authors fear being kept out of the gate for life". I am hesitant to accept this observation as providing a true reflection of the politics of scholarship in South Africa. This is because scientific publications on earth are incalculable. If one is indeed "kept out of the gate" of a particular journal, there is always a possibility of the affected author submitting his/her article for publication consideration in another scientific publishing outlet, which may even be more serious and respectable (Koorts, 2016). So Sebola's claim is outlandish as it seeks to imply that there is a "generally corrupt relationship" or unethical collusion among all journal editors in a particular discipline or across the disciplines.

For Sebola (2018:6) "… some mounting evidence suggests that personal differences in opinions between authors and editors have a direct bearing on the acceptability or unacceptability of the article in a publication controlled by specific editors in academic circles". This may be true, but not very common. I have personally experienced the bitter side of it with the *African Journal of Public Affairs (AJPA)* and the *International Journal of African Renaissance Studies (IJARS)* (Sesanti, 2018). The former journal has in fact given the author of the article under review a special treatment for quite some time, obviously for reasons that are best known to Sebola and its *(AJPA)* editor (Kuye, 2017). At the time of writing this chapter, Sebola and the editor of *AJPA* were both full professors in Public Administration at the university in Limpopo, South Africa. As such, it is interesting to note Sebola's (2018:4) submission that "editors are responsible for ensuring that author's feedback is compulsory". But my encounter with the editor of *AJPA* suggests that this journal discreetly deviates from this undertaking. As hinted above, it is common knowledge that *AJPA* is edited by Sebola's colleague. As such, the widening chasm between Sebola's scholarly postulations and actions on the academic landscape warrants that he be reminded of the English adage that "if you cannot take punches, do not throw punches".

Scholarly peer review in South Africa

Emphatically, Sebola have qualms with the editors' perceived or real upper hand in the validation or invalidation of the process of peer review. Again, validity on qualitative studies of the peer review process and politics of scholarship in Africa is a debatable issue (Sithole, 2009; Shai, 2016). That certain editors manipulate manuscript scoring or assessment in favour of some and against some qualifies as a speculation;

unless Sebola is writing from personal experience as an editor in his own right. Other than this, his speculation should be treated as such or should simply be equated to an elusive truth. That is because his insinuation cannot be proven beyond reasonable doubt, more especially because most journals in South Africa and beyond are moving towards the online submission and review system that also provide a secure platform for the reviewer to write comments for the author that are separate from those meant for the attention of the editor.

That the manner of using peer review to determine the quality of scholarship is questionable remains a tired narrative, which has been previously enunciated by scholars such as Sithole (2009) and Ngobeni (2010). In spite of Sebola's (2018:1) reservations about scientific peer review, he commends it for "its ability to detect fraud before publication". While this commendation has elements of truth, it is equally debatable. For example, the functions of literature review in research reflect that no idea is purely new (Shai, 2016). In the same line of reasoning, Leedy and Ormrod (2013: 51) enunciated that:

> Those who have conducted research before you belong to a community of scholars, each of whom has journeyed into the unknown to bring back an insight, a truth, [and] a point of light. What they have recorded of their journeys and findings will make it easier for you to explore the unknown: to help you also discover an insight, a truth, or a point of light.

Besides the foregoing argument, "turn it in" plagiarism software comes handy in this regard and many serious and reputable journals makes use of it to detect academic fraud. Normally, a higher similarity index in a manuscript article will cause it to be rejected at the editorial desk, before it can even be send for a thorough external peer review. It is for this reason that internal peer review is important for any journal, to avoid an unfortunate situation wherein the precious time of often busy academics is wasted in peer reviewing sloppy manuscripts which do not have a potential for publication. The foregoing observation represents an antithesis of Sebola's (2018:5) conviction that "no idea is not a good idea as long as the editor has a good sense of disseminating the author's idea to the people". This conviction may be partially true, but it fails to acknowledge the fact that the goodness of a research idea cannot be used to disregard the importance of its proper conceptualisation and contextualisation (Gumede, 2019).

To add, it is important to note that unlike popular literature in the form of newspapers (Maserumule, 2011), scientific journals are normally not meant for general readership. Each and every journal has a targeted scientific community of readers within a particular discipline and/or related disciplines. Therefore, it is important for any author to familiarise himself/herself with the scope and readership of his/her targeted journal, to avoid a situation wherein his/her article would be rejected at the editorial desk. The responsibility of aligning an article orientation to a scope and readership of a particular journal can never be the primary responsibility of editors and an attempt to apportion blame on them for failure to do that is tantamount to an attempt to abuse their humanity. Authors who do not have an appetite to conform to the scope and expectations of the readership of their targeted journal may be lost in the terrain of scientific writing and therefore, they should consider resorting to literary writing. However, my experience about literary writing also informs me that it has its own conventions which are hardly overlooked during the process of peer review. The identified typologies of peer review in this article suggest that there is indeed no universally acceptable/ uniform approach to the elevation of the quality of manuscripts.

While we may blame the old guard for refusing to learn, we equally draw solace from the English adage: "you cannot teach an old dog new tricks". However, this adage can be counter-balanced through a Sotho expression: *"thuto ga e tšofallwe"*. This expression denotes that where there is will, learning is possible even at an old age stage of life. As it is important for all of us to remind the old guard that learning is a life-long process, we must also be cautious about the danger of resurrecting epistemologically decentred or dead-hood from the ashes of coloniality (Nnadozie, 2015). Thus giving them a second chance of epistemological life might be abused to reverse the few Afrocentric gains that we have achieved overtime.

Among the three types of peer review identified by Sebola (2018:3), he contends that "emerging journals in developing countries may not be allowed to follow" single blind review model as they may be accused in certain quarters for not rigorously upholding scientific quality promotion and enhancement principles. I argue that only the advocates of white supremacy in academy are still stubbornly treating journals and scholarship produced in the developing world (i.e. Africa) with contempt (Gumede, 2019). This tendency cannot be delinked from the general tendency in the mainstream international media to demonise and criminalise the Africans and the colonised (Shai, 2012).

In his usual spirit of doubting the competence of journals in non-industrialised world, Sebola (2018:4) is of the view that upcoming journals in developing countries that experiment with open peer review risk being "removed from the list of credible journal indexing institutions". Depending on currency, strategic and tactical importance of the issue being dissected, the *Journal of Public Affairs (JPA)* sometimes uses open peer review, but in a safer way (Losbanes, 2018). In the case of *JPA*, authors and reviewers' names are not revealed to each other. But the authors are given an option to nominate or reject possible reviewers. Such a nomination must be coupled with reasons for the author's preference of a particular reviewer or rejection thereof. While this system is conducive for the prevention of scholarly prejudice, the journal still reserves the right to accept or reject the author's nomination of peer reviewers. Relatedly, Sebola's (2018:4) contention is that "single and open peer review may not be a good model to follow considering the commercial route academic publishing is taking today". The commercial route followed in certain circles of the contemporary academic publishing cannot be delinked from the overall societal corporatisation (Shai, 2017). Such a corporatisation has much to do with the forceful imposition of the business model on universities which is the by-product of the manifestations of the wanton, brutal and inhuman capitalism in the society (Mbeki, 2009). Meanwhile, a third main type of peer review identified by Sebola (2018) is the one that involves two reviewers, which is popularly known as "double blind peer review".

In South Africa, some journals have since embraced the recommendation of Academy of Science of South Africa (ASAAf) thereby extending the double blind peer review into triple blind peer review (Phago, 2018). This model has been propagated with the understanding of the possibility of two blind reviewers to deadlock by arriving at fundamentally different recommendations on a particular manuscript. Like editors, reviewers are humans. Under no circumstances could their envisaged impartiality be exaggerated. Contrary to a popular belief, under normal circumstances it is uncommon for two great reviewers/ thinkers to think alike. It is for this reason that the voice of the majority would prevail in a triple blind peer review. The pioneers of the triple blind review are supposedly under the impression that journal editors have a limited role (if there is any) during the process of external peer review.

Delinking *politricks* [politics] from the realities of scientific editorship

It is correctly pointed out by Sebola (2018) that *Journal of Public Administration (JOPA)* is owned by South African Association of Public Administration and Management (SAAPAM), a scholarly and professional association of Public Administration in South Africa. However, it is instructive for the reader to note that for the many years that Sebola has served as a national board member of SAAPAM until May 2018, he has never formerly and/or openly registered the alleged editorial misconduct by Mashupye H. Maserumule, the editor of *JOPA*. It is common knowledge within SAAPAM that Sebola's presidential ambitions of the same organisation were thwarted during the year 2017 annual general meeting in Empangeni, Kwazulu Natal. Subsequently, his membership of SAAPAM was terminated through the consensus of the national board after he was proven to have hopelessly failed to execute his fiduciary duties and working against the mission and vision of the same organisation. By implication, his ordinary membership of SAAPAM was also suspended (Khalo, 2018). Sebola now laments (in the article under review) his concerns after the above two major imperatives in his relationship with SAAPAM raises more questions than answers.

Moreover, a majority of his publications appears in the SAAPAM owned *JOPA*. These are the very publications that parachuted him to the status of "full professorship" at the university in Limpopo. If Sebola's allegations about *JOPA* and its current editor are anything to go by; then it is safe to state that his article in *KOERS* has a clandestine mischievous agenda. Any thought of lending credence to his claims would suggest the urgent need for some academic promotions (i.e. un-professorial professors) at the university in Limpopo and beyond to be revisited (Tshikwatamba, 2008). In his article, Sebola (2018) borrows from Klenert and Wager (2010: 1) to make a point that journal editors are expected to "adhere to universal standards and practices". I argue that this is a cheap and outdated requirement because descriptions such as universal standards only exist in theory and not practice (Welsing, 1991). The standards and practices that have been projected in certain circles as universal are in fact, Euro-American standards (Asante, 2003). Among others, such standards entail the notion that is termed "objective evaluation". Relatedly, Sebola (2018:3) asserts that "the expert is an individual who is mostly trusted by the editor in objective evaluation of scientific material". This conception is problematic especially when it is propagated by him. Hence, there are previous instances when some of my articles submitted to him for publication consideration in either SAAPAM-Limpopo Chapter or International Conference on Public Administration and Development Alternatives (IPADA) proceedings were allocated to non-experts for review; some of them emanating from the discipline of Information Studies at my university. The jury is out there to test whether this practice in any way nearer to ethical conduct or not, at least within the context of peer review in the discipline of Public Administration and other cognate disciplines.

As an extension of the qualitative research paradigm, Afrocentricity's pioneers educate us that what is often presented to us as objective is nothing but the inter-subjectivities of the privileged and powerful group of scholars who have been immersed on the value systems of the white society (Welsing, 1991). Objectivity as envisaged by Sebola (2018) has limited space in African scholarship. The forgoing analysis should be understood within the context that as a quality criterion, objectivity is derived from ethos that are foreign to the Africans and Africa (Milam, 1992). Concepts such as objectivity can never be neutral. At their thrust is the survival of Caucasians and the uncritical acceptance or use of loaded concepts such as objectivity. This is tantamount to an affirmation of the white ways of life; which are mostly not good for Africans (Shai, 2016). Instead of African scholars such as Sebola being obsessed with objectivity or hiding behind its veil to discredit well-established traditions of peer review, he ought to intellectually find himself and epistemologically relocate to Africa thereby embracing descriptions such as trustworthiness and reliability as the quality criteria for his thinking, analysis and writing (Milam, 1992). Objectivity as an imbued quality criterion is contextually illegitimate when it comes to the study of African issues, in Africa, by Africans and for people of African descent (Hilliard III, 1999). If African scholars and others from the South easily and recklessly embrace such descriptions as objectivity, they are likely to be boxed by the Caucasians and ultimately lose the intellectual warfare

(Asante, 2003). Of concern is that, we already have senior African scholars who have unconsciously joined the intellectual warfare in support of the Caucasians (Carruthers, 1999). It is therefore important for interventions like the current chapter to be widely spread so that the lost ground in terms of the intellectual warfare can be regained.

Conclusion

This chapter can be summed up through an English adage that: "If you live in glass house do not throw stones". The fundamental factual, editorial and substantive errors in the article under review, which was authored by Sebola (2018) vindicates my distaste for ethical embarrassment in certain scholarly publications like his piece. This observation should not be unnecessarily sensationalised because being a scholar entails calling things by their proper names. No amount of blame game between the editor of the journal where this article was published and its author (Sebola) can exempt the latter from his primary responsibility to strive for sound intellectual direction, rigour and/or clarity of thought. The notion of "publish or perish" does not also qualify as an excuse for the poor quality of the article under review. This is because its author is already a full professor and Acting Director of the School of Economics and Management at the university in Limpopo (Shai, 2019). In this chapter, I have deliberately problematised the quality of the article under review with a full consciousness that quality is sacrosanct (Manyaka, 2016). But its basics are known by all serious and respectable scholars. It has been established that activism scholarship may be career limiting and I add that this is also observable in certain South African universities wherein applications for academic promotion by activist scholars are often unfairly treated by powerful managers, individually and collectively. This form of academic toxicity is driven by the desperate desire to sensor assertive and independent academics and to foster blind loyalty within their ranks. This is a clear attack on freedom of association and expression, particularly in respect of academic freedom (Ray, 2016). The foregoing analysis is well-captured by Mekoa (2016) when he outlined the challenges facing Black African academics in South African universities as including jealousy, managerial dictatorship, ethnic chauvinism, *broerskap* [and *sisterskap*] (my addition). In this case, I am reminded of one research professor at the university in Limpopo who has covertly expressed reservations about the institution's annual

Vice Chancellor's Research Excellence award system. While his reservations are shared by some, their underlying reasons are purely non-academic, but personal. That a young, Black and Afrocentric scholar collectively causes them atrocious pains of having to swallow their bitterness, as per Chinese expression.

Recommendations and way forward

In the final analysis, a key lesson that can be drawn from the above discussion is that in certain academic spaces in South Africa, prolific publishing by young African scholars can be dangerous and in fact, it can cause them to perish. In such academically polluted spaces, blind loyalty is more rewarding than academic excellence. In this context, if you publish impressively you cause some insecurities for some old managers with questionable academic credentials that one wonders how they became professors. When line managers are threatened by their subordinates, personal and professional relations are bound to deteriorate to a point wherein enabling conditions for academic excellence often dissipate. Thus, such a coterie of old managers who are self-confessed professors tend to reward a mixture of academic laziness and blind loyalty at the expense of academic excellence in relation to their subordinates. I argue that a combination of all of the above factors is at the centre of the demoralisation of academics, which in turn serve as a dangerous recipe for the dearth of scientific knowledge in South Africa.

References

Asante, M.K. 2003. Afrocentricity: *The Theory of Social Change*. Chicago: African American Images.
Azibo, D.A. 2011. Understanding Essentialism as Fundamental: The Centred African Perspective on the Nature of Prototypical Human Nature- Cosmological Ka (Spirit). *The Western Journal of Black Studies*, Vol 35 (2): 77-91.
Baylis, J., Smith, S. & Owens, P (eds). 2008. The *Globalization of World Politics: An Introduction to International Relations*. (4th Ed). New York: Oxford University Press.

Boahen, A.A. (Ed). 2003. *General History of Africa-VII: Africa Under Colonial Domination 1880-1935* (Abridged Ed). Glosderry: New Africa Education.

Carruthers, J.H. 1999. *Intellectual Warfare*. Chicago: Third World Press.

Chazan, N. 1988. *Politics and Society in Contemporary Africa*. Basingstoke: Macmillan.

Hilliard III, A.G. 1999. *SBA: The Reawakening of the African Mind*. Florida: Makare Publishing Company.

Gumede, V. 2019. Is there a doctor in the house? We need more PhD graduates. *Daily Maverick*. https://www.dailymaverick.co.za/opinionista/ 2019-11-13-is-the re-a-doctor-in-the-house-we-need-more-phd-gradu ate s/ (Accessed 13 November 2019).

Hussein, A. 1998. Kwame Nkrumah: Leninist Tzar or Leninist Garvey. In O.H. Kokole (ed), *The Global African: A Portrait of Ali A. Mazrui*. Trenton: Africa World Press.

Lekane, G.M. & Asuelime, L. 2017. One country, three colonial legacies: The politics of colonialism, capitalism and development in pre- and post- colonial Cameroon. *Journal for Contemporary History*, Vol 42 (1): 134-153.

Losbanes, L.C. (Ed). 2018. Manuscripts I Have Co-Authored. *Journal of Public Affairs*, https:mc.manuscriptcentral.com/jpa (accessed 10 June 2018).

Khalo, T. 2018. Termination of SAAPAM membership. A letter from the SAAPAM national board to Professor MP Sebola, 20 June 2018.

Klenert, S. & Wager, E. 2010. Responsible research publication: international standards for editor. A position statement developed at the 2nd world conference on research integrity in a global environment. Imperial College Press/ World Scientific Publishing, Singapore: 3-28.

Koorts, L. 2016. Re: Manuscript. An email message from *Historia*'s Editor in Chief to authors (name withheld for ethical reasons).

Kuye, J. (Ed). 2017. *African Journal of Public Affairs*, Vol 9 (5): i-210.

Macupe, B. 2019. Report finds most SA universities well run. *Mail & Guardian*, 15-21 November 2019.

Manyaka, R.K. 2016. Book Review- Local Government Administration in Post-Apartheid South Africa: Some Critical Perspectives, MP Sebola (Ed.). *Journal of Public Administration*, Vol 51 (3): 436-441.

Maserumule, M.H. 2011. Good Governance in the New Partnership for Africa's Development (NEPAD: A Public Administration

Perspective. Unpublished PhD Thesis. Pretoria: University of South Africa.

Maserumule, M.H. 2015a. Engaged Scholarship and Liberatory Science: A Professoriate, Mount Grace, and SAAPAM in the Decoloniality Mix. *Journal of Public Administration*, Vol 50 (2): 200-222.

Maserumule, M.H. 2015b. Why Africa's professors are afraid of colonial education being dismantled. *Mail & Guardian*, http://mg.co.za/article/2015-11-26-why-africas-professors-are-afraid-of-colonial-education-being-dismantled (Accessed 26 November 2015).

Mazama, A. (Ed). 2003. *The Afrocentric Paradigm*. Trenton: Africa World Press.

Mbeki, M. 2009. *Architects of Poverty: Why Africa's Capitalism Needs Changing*. Johannesburg: Pan Macmillan.

Mekoa, I. 2016. *Silent No More: Challenges Facing Black African Academics at South African Universities*. Cape Town: The Incwadi Press.

Leedy, P.D. & Ormrod, J.E. 2013. *Practical Research: Planning and Design*. Boston: Pearson.

Ndlovu-Gatsheni, S.J. 2018. The Dynamics of Epistemological Freedom. *Strategic Review of Southern Africa*, Vol 40(1):16-45.

Ngobeni, S. (Ed) 2010. *Scholarly Publishing in Africa: Opportunities and Impediments*. Pretoria: Africa Institute of South Africa.

Nkuna, V.M. & Shai, K.B. 2018. An exploration of the 2016 violent protests in Vuwani, Limpopo province of South Africa. *Man in India*, Vol 98 (3): 425-436.

Nnadozie, U.O. 2015. Coloniality and Governance in Africa in the Twenty-First Century: The Challenges of Public Administration. *Journal of Public Administration*, Vol 50 (2): 191-199.

Phago, K.G. 2018. Briefing on Editorial (JOPA) issues. SAAPAM National Board Meeting, Tshwane University of Technology, Soshanguve Campus, 23 November 2018.

Ray, M. 2016. *Free Fall: Why South African Universities are in a Race Against Time*. Johannesburg: Bookstorm.

Reviere, R. 2001. Toward an Afrocentric research methodology. *Journal of Black Studies*, Vol 31 (6): 709-728.

Sebola M.P. 2018. Peer review, scholarship and editors of scientific publications: the death of scientific knowledge in Africa. *KOERS-Bulletin for Christian Scholarship*, Vol 83 (1):1-13.

Sesanti, S. 2018. *International Journal of African Renaissance Studies* – RARS-2017-0007 has been withdrawn. An email message from the Deputy Editor to author (name withheld for ethical reasons), 14 February 2018.

Shai, K.B. 2009. *Rethinking United States-South Africa Relations*. Hoedspruit: Royal B. Foundation.

Shai K.B. 2012. "Africa as a threat to the national security of the US: Unpacking claims and realities", in *Peace and Security for African Development*, Proceedings of the sixth annual AISA Young Graduates and Scholars (AYGS) Conference, Boksburg, South Africa, 23-26 March 2011.

Shai K.B. 2016. An Afrocentric Critique of the United States of America's foreign policy towards Africa: The case studies of Ghana and Tanzania, 1990-2014. Unpublished PhD Thesis. Sovenga: University of Limpopo.

Shai K.B. 2017. South African State Capture: A Symbiotic Affair between Business and State Going Bad (?). *Insight on Africa*, Vol 9 (1): 1-14.

Shai K.B, Molapo R.R. & Sodi T. 2017. The United States of America's post-1990 foreign policy towards West Africa: The case study of Ghana. *Journal for Contemporary History*, Vol 42 (1): 154-173.

Shai K.B. 2019. The death of scientific knowledge in [South] Africa: An Afrocentric response to M.P. Sebola. *Journal of Public Affairs*. e1975. https://doi.org/10.1002/pa.1975

Sithole M.P. 2009. *Unequal Peers*. Pretoria: Africa Institute of South Africa.

Stafford T. 2016. How liars create 'the illusion of truth'. *BBC* (online). http://www.bbc.com/future/story/20161026-how-liars-create-the-illusion-of-truth (accessed 26 October 2016).

Tshikwatamba N.E. (2008, October 24). Letter to Dr Sebola in response to several matters.

Welsing F.C. 1991. The ISIS Papers: The keys to the Colours. Washington, D.C: CW Publishing.

CHAPTER THREE

Mokoko Sebola on 'Scientific Knowledge in Africa': An Afrocentric Critique

Introduction

The subject of the politics of scholarship in Africa and beyond remains under-researched. This situation can be largely attributed to the fact that there are very few scholars (if any) who specialise in the politics of scholarship (Ngobeni, 2010; Sithole, 2009). Those who research and write about the politics of scholarship come from traditional academic disciplines such as Political Science, Public Administration and Sociology. Such scholars who dare to venture into this discourse are often pinned with labels such as activist or anarchist scholar. The negative connotations often attached to the meaning and essence of these labels has rendered the subject of the politics of scholarship unappealing to most scholars. Even as and when they do work in this regard, it tends to be on an ad hoc basis. It is also instructive for the reader to note that globally, there are very few (if any) institutions of higher learning that provide tuition in the politics of scholarship. Nonetheless, issues pertinent to the politics of scholarship are at times touched on in passing in the knowledge exchange mediums within academic fields such as Global Political Economy, Public Policy Analysis and Information Studies (Shai, 2017). One of the few scholars who have recently added their voices to the subject in South Africa is Mokoko P. Sebola. His contribution has appeared in *KOERS-Bulletin for Christian Scholarship*. The central argument of his contribution is that "the manner in which the scholarship peer review as a process is conducted and perceived in the editorial arena is a cause of insufficient knowledge production in Africa" (Sebola, 2018:1). The two papers entitled "The death of scientific knowledge in [South] Africa: An Afrocentric response to MP Sebola" (Shai, 2019a) and "[Un]masking *Sebola*'s mythology on the politics of scholarship in South Africa: An Afrocentric youth perspective" (Shai, 2019b) represent a preliminary anti-thesis to Sebola's thesis. Against this backdrop, the current [and/or 3rd] chapter aim to employ Afrocentricity as an alternative theoretical and contextual lens to critique Sebola's piece, which is slightly misleading.

Professor Mokoko Sebola and His Status in the Knowledge Industry

Professor Mokoko Sebola is a recognisable figure within the Public Administration fraternity in South Africa. At the time of writing this chapter, Sebola was a Professor of Public Administration and Acting Director of the School of Economics and Management at the university in Limpopo, South Africa (University of Limpopo, 2018). He is also an editor of the *Journal of Public Administration and Development Alternatives* (JPADA), which is owned and managed by his relatively unknown company, Batalea Publishers (Manyaka, 2016). Although not listed among South African Post-Secondary Education (SAPSE) accredited journals, *JPADA* enjoys a closer relationship with Sebola's flagship project, the International Conference on Public Administration and Development Alternatives (IPADA). IPADA should not be confused with the newly established and promising Institute for Preservation and Development (IPAD). Equally important, IPADA and JPADA do not have any relationship whatsoever with the prestigious *Journal of Public Administration* (JoPA), which is produced and owned by the South African Association of Public Administration and Management (SAAPAM) (Maserumule, 2015a; Khalo, 2018). IPAD is a non-profit organisation with a focus on the Limpopo province but is headquartered in the city of Tshwane (Pretoria), the administrative capital of South Africa. In terms of academic training, Sebola holds a Doctor of Technology (Public Management) from Tshwane University of Technology (TUT). However, he is largely grounded in Educational and Tourism Studies, a critical factor that often causes him to miss the basics (concepts, theories and current debates) in Public Administration as evidenced in most of his conference presentations and scientific writings (Tshikwatamba, 2008). Despite this observable weakness, he tends to position himself as a 'pro' when it comes to scholarship matters, simply because he operates in spaces wherein the culture of research and publishing is not yet deeply rooted (Manyaka, 2016).

Conceptualising and Contextualising the Theory of Afrocentricity

The politics of scholarship in Africa has been a subject of relatively few studies, most of which are Eurocentric in theory and method (Muchie & Baskaran, 2013). It is on this basis that I foreground my chapter on Afrocentric theory and paradigm as articulated by Asante (2003). I also draw from like-minded Afrocentric scholars such as Azibo (2011), Mazama (2003) and Mekoa (2016). In this chapter, Afrocentricity is understood as the mode of thought and action in which the centrality of African interests, values and perspectives predominate. In this context, it is placing African people and experiences at the centre of the analysis of the politics of scholarship in Africa, which is equally poised to serve as an attack on the falsification of truth in the Sebola piece under review. Two main propositions of Afrocentricity are worth outlining: (1) It is primarily pan-Africanist; (2) It is central to the development of new concepts and directions (Asante, 2003). As such, Afrocentricity was chosen as a theoretical and contextual lens for this chapter due to its dual cognitive and functional roles. This does not mean that it is the only theory that wields the capacity to critique the politics of scholarship in Africa. However, the key issue behind the introduction of Afrocentricity in this chapter is to also appeal for its acknowledgment and acceptance within scholarly circles as one voice among many. Having said this, Afrocentricity was also an unavoidable choice for me. Since I am African seeking to understand the politics of scholarship in Africa, Afrocentricity becomes a non-negotiable epistemological identity for me and any attempt to deviate from this has a potential to produce gross transversal errors in the operationalisation of the research for this chapter (Carruthers, 1999). Contrary to the falsified claims and notions of objectivity in the Eurocentric thought system, Afrocentricity also appreciates the reality that "the research process is a balance between the researcher expertise, the benefit of an outsider perspective and the main direction given by the elders" (Khupe & Keane, 2017: 31). The foregoing observation vindicates my long held belief that Sebola's thesis can be well understood when linked to his 'being' and hence, the necessity to provide facts [and healing truths] about his status in the knowledge industry.

Africa's Scientific Knowledge in Perspective: An overview

Contemporary studies reveal that Africa does not contribute more than 2% of the global scientific knowledge (Sebola, 2018). Much of this 2% emanates from South Africa and to a certain extent, Egypt. The poor performance of Africa in contrast to other continents when it comes to the production and dissemination of scientific knowledge cannot be delinked from the unequal economic power relations between them (Shai, 2017). This premise is also applicable to a comparative study of South Africa and Egypt's contribution of scientific knowledge against that coming from other African countries, most of which are developing nations. While South Africa is also considered a developing country in certain circles, for the purpose of this chapter it is considered to be in a transition zone between a developing and industrialised nation. Because of South Africa's upper hand in the global race from the production and dissemination of scientific knowledge when compared with its African counterparts, a discussion of this nature is bound to be centred on Africa and ultimately zero in on South Africa.

Contextually, Sebola (2018) apportions blame for what he terms the "death" of scientific knowledge in Africa to the editors and their peer review processes and mechanisms. Sebola's decision to resort to simplistic explanations to complex problems is nothing but an unguided and arrogant academic move. Firstly, the analogy of death to explain the state of scientific knowledge is misplaced and it lacks a proper context. In quantitative terms, it can only be fair to compare the state of scientific knowledge in Africa with other continents that have a similar colonial history (Shai, 2016). Qualitatively, the bashing of the current state of Africa's scientific knowledge as insufficient lacks an appreciation of the stolen legacy of Africa's scientific innovations by Europe (James, 1954). It is also not clear as to what Africa's scientific knowledge is insufficient for. If this has to do with societal impact, the reality of the knowledge industry in the global landscape reflects that even in countries that are well rated for abundantly producing and disseminating scientific knowledge, much of their inventions have in fact contributed to a creation and sustenance of earthly problems in certain parts of the world (Shai, 2012). Globalisation and its attendant interdependence imply that the failure of any scientific knowledge to generate solutions for societal problems in one part of the world risks the spiralling of such problems to all corners of the globe, a situation that policy analysts term spill over effects. As such, the serious effects of the failure to produce scientific knowledge that solves real societal problems on the global scale can best be summed up through the analogy of the "tragedy of the commons" (Baylis, Smith & Owens, 2008). This is the case even when it comes to high impact factor journals or articles that are extensively cited. This does not necessarily provide a true reflection of the quality of a particular scholarly contribution. The key issue is that a known network of scholars tends to cite each other's work and avoid extensive citing of those works whose authors are outside their network. Relatedly, it is not correct that every work enlisted under the references of a particular manuscript have in fact been read in totality by its author. Inclusion of a particular work in the reference list of his/her article is driven by a number of reasons that are beyond the scope of this chapter, some of which are centred on the promotion of each other's work. It is for this reason that some scholars have a tendency to deliberately omit references of the works authored by those they personally disagree with, even though such contribution might have shaped their manuscripts in several ways. This unethical conduct is also observed in Sebola's piece (2018). Secondly, it cannot be correct to reduce the seemingly non-impressive scientific knowledge generation of a diverse continent such as Africa to a single factor (Chazan, 1988). The manner in which scientific editors handle peer review may be a manifestation of a particular problem in the knowledge industry, but it cannot be a sole root cause of low scientific knowledge generation of Africa, which is multi-layered and multi-dimensional by its very nature. The foregoing observation denotes that the problem of low scientific knowledge generation in Africa is complex and involves the interplay of several inter-related political, socio-economic and/or technological factors.

Moral contract between scholars and the academic community

A breakdown in the moral contract between academics and institutions of higher learning in Africa, particularly in South Africa, is at the centre of the low scientific knowledge generation and dissemination. Editors have a small role in the escalation of this problem. The major weakness of those who have a different view, like Sebola (2018), is their desperate desire to understand a present situation as dictated by the immediate conditions. The best way to approach this discourse is to locate it within a historical context. This observation dovetails with the English expression that "the river which does not know its source dries quickly". This assertion must be understood within the context that scientific writing is not an inborn talent but a skill that one has to learn, particularly through post-graduate studies, which entail research proposal/report writing. However, this stage of academic life is often riddled with unethical practices that are perpetuated by supervisors and/or any person whom an emerging scholar looks up to for academic mentorship and support (Earl-Taylor, 2018).

In South Africa, for example, it is not uncommon to hear or read about young scholars' complaints about academic bullying by their seniors. Related to this, I am reminded of an email written to Professor Sebola by a young colleague, Rasodi K. Manyaka, shortly after he resigned from the university in Limpopo and subsequently joined TUT. In his email, he stated:

> I felt compelled to write to you in order to put the matter of my co-supervision of Matlala's thesis to rest. I am writing this email to respectfully request you to reinstate my name as a co-supervisor of the student before the student's work could be published online. My efforts into the student's work should be respected and acknowledged (Manyaka 2017).

The email extract above insinuates an extreme case of intellectual dishonesty and academic theft, whose recurrence (if not arrested) has a potential to demoralise the complainant to a point wherein he would no longer take further research supervision responsibilities elsewhere. These are serious issues that can have a long-term effect on a young scholar's interests and passion on the research enterprise as a whole. This is because such bad experiences in the early stages of an academic career are not good. Having said this, it is instructive for the reader to note that the university in Limpopo does not have a monopoly over challenges of this nature. If recent media reports are anything to go by, it would appear that the University of Fort Hare (UFH) is also plagued by such serious unethical practices that are perpetuated by those operating from a position of privilege and administrative power (Earl-Taylor, 2018). It is worth noting that the negative ramifications of unethical conduct hinted above do not only affect young academics who are involved in supervision, but also serve as a time bomb for frustrating post-graduate students, ultimately causing them to lose interest in furthering post-graduate studies. This premise should be understood within the context that students are often caught in the crossfires of petty conflicts between academic colleagues. Based on the extract above and my personal encounters with Sebola, he is clearly not fit to enter into a discourse of judgement as evidenced in his article under review. In fact, Sebola is not new to shenanigans that harm the very academic infrastructure that has been put in place in the new democratic dispensation for the purposes of supporting present and future academics in making meaningful contributions to the production and dissemination of scientific knowledge. The thwarting of his SAAPAM presidential ambitions in 2017 in Empangeni, KwaZulu-Natal province of South Africa has left him aggrieved. Subsequently, 2018 saw him abusing his managerial powers to make it impossible for his subordinates to attend future SAAPAM conferences. Such an attitude proves a popular notion about his selfishness and self-centredness when it comes to academic conferences and publication opportunities. It is on this basis that in 2018, his narrow political agenda within the discipline of Public Administration to trample on his subordinates' right to attend SAAPAM conferences, which undoubtedly serve as a peer review platform and a capacity-building intervention in terms of scientific writing, presentation and publication (Khalo, 2018).

Academic promotion: A mechanism of patronage or reward?

Another factor that has a deleterious effect on the morality of African scholars or their urge to publish extensively is academic managerial dictatorship and the conflation of university management and council's roles in the manner in which applications for academic promotion are handled in certain institutions of higher learning in South Africa. In this context, I am reminded of the unfair and inconsistent manner in which an application by a young South African scholar for promotion from a Senior Lecturer to Associate Professor was handled at a certain university in South Africa during the 2018 academic year. According to this university's policy on academic promotion, which is also expressed in its job adverts that are in the public domain, at least five research articles in South African Post-Secondary Education (SAPSE) accredited journals is a mandatory requirement for an application for promotion to Associate

Professorship. Interestingly, in the case referred to above, the applicant filed his application in January 2018, with 13 research articles in SAPSE-accredited journals plus subsidy-earning book chapters and monographs. This application was recommended by the relevant faculty and subsequently given a nod by the internal and external board of assessors. The latter involves subject experts. Normally, final feedback on application of this nature is provided within six months. In this case, a final but incoherent feedback was provided after 12 months and following several requests from different angles including the labour union. To the shock of the applicant, his application was not endorsed by the university council, through its Human Resources Committee. Two main reasons were reported by the university management as the basis for the decision of the council not to endorse his application: undeveloped post-graduate student supervision record and lack of self-management skills. It is argued that the manifestation of this case is reflective of unfair labour practice and discrimination. This is because the university in question's policy on academic promotion is not clear about the quantity or quality of post-graduate supervision credentials required for promotion at this level, a loophole that is often exploited to disadvantage other colleagues who may not be in the good books of certain influential senior managers at the university. The foregoing assertion is informed by the fact that the application under consideration was supported by over 15 supervised and completed research reports including one for a Masters' degree. To add, precedence was laid at this institution wherein academics without impeccable post-graduate student supervision credentials were promoted to either Associate or Full Professorship. To make matters worse, some academics were recently promoted even before they reached mandatory minimum requirements in terms of journal articles. The university under review's policy on academic promotion is also silent about personal management, a very factor which is at times invoked to shoot down applications of those who are deemed to be vocal or assertive.

Contextually, it is my well-considered view that in the new democratic dispensation, there ought to be a clear separation between management and council powers. Under normal circumstances, matters pertaining to academic promotion ought to be a management function, while the council simply plays an oversight role. But in the context of the academic promotion application under review, it would appear that there is a clear conflation of roles between management and council, a situation which represents bad for corporate governance especially as it relates to institutions that have been favoured with autonomy by law. Such conflation of roles between management and council/boards is also rife within most of South Africa's state-owned enterprises.

If this is anything to go by, it is safe to argue that the policy on academic promotion at the university under study and related legislative framework is not applied consistently. This is a sad situation that leaves room for the abuse of promotion policy to reward blind loyalty at the expense of academic excellence. Although often downplayed, such tendencies have a serious effect in the death of scientific knowledge in Africa and South Africa in particular. Considering the moral breakdown among leaders in different sectors of South Africa, it may not be far-fetched to assert that the university under study does not have a monopoly in the perpetuation of *broerskap*, jealousy and nepotism in the manner in which applications for academic promotion are handled (Mekoa, 2016). It is equally painstaking when such unfairness finds expression in historically black universities, which are well known as among many of the country's sites of the struggle for liberation from the inhumane and brutal system of apartheid under the National Party (NP) (Shai, 2009). It is for this reason that, despite their potential, most historically black universities in South Africa are still lagging behind in terms of global research ranking and, implicitly, being on a self-reduction trajectory to become glorified high schools with an obsession with teaching to the detriment of other core businesses of a real university (Ray, 2016).

Emerging from the above, it is clear that scientific review of applications for academic promotion, article manuscripts and applications for National Research Foundation (NRF) rating is a hotly contested terrain in the knowledge industry. Considering the fact that there is no alternative to it, I argue that criticising it without proposing measures in terms of how best it can be improved is a futile exercise. The aforementioned argument dovetails with Mafeje's (as cited by Nabudere, 2010:11) submission that "Africa is the worst victim of intellectual and cultural imperialism and consequently is in the grips of the worst development crisis ever. And yet, no clear views have emerged from African intellectuals as to how the situation could be remedied". Perhaps expertise of retirees should be re-sourced for the purpose of doing scientific reviews and the government through agencies such as the

National Research Foundation (NRF), and the National Institute of Humanities and Social Sciences (NIHSS) should devise a means through which retirees who are assisting the knowledge industry with credible scientific reviews can be incentivised. Such is likely to create an enabling environment wherein applicants/authors of manuscripts receive constructive/meaningful review feedback without any form of prejudice.

While unfairness is institutionalised in the handling of scientific reviews, it is equally worse or systemised in certain quarters. For example, NRF and a number of universities in South Africa emphasise the need to publish in international journals. But their conception of an 'international' journal is problematic. It tends to imply journals published outside of the African continent. This is a serious flaw in their scientific reviews because, in essence, international denotes 'across the border'. Therefore, the exclusion of journals published in either Botswana, Ghana and/or Nigeria as international is factually wrong and its explanation has much to do with stubborn legacies of coloniality (Nnadozie, 2015). In this colonial matrix, our epistemology is not only rejected by our European and North-American counterparts, but its very existence is challenged by the home- (African) based disciples of coloniality and knowledge imperialism (Nkuna & Shai, 2018). Sebola's (2018:10) invocation that "fighting anyone with an alternative knowledge characterises the scientific publication in all journals" is hyperbolic. While this may be true for selected journals, there is no sound basis for this premise to be generalised. Having said this, I would concede that his invocation finds true and honest expression in the *Nordic Journal of African Studies* (NJAS), *International Journal of African Renaissance Studies* (IJARS) and *Historia*, just to mention a few (Koorts, 2016; Koivu, 2017; Katto, 2017). IJARS attaches scholarly value to certain individuals and institutions and for it, the processing of contributions from historically disadvantaged universities is an act of charity (Sesanti, 2018). On the other hand, *Historia* is owned and produced by the Historical Association of South Africa (HASA), which is still fundamentally untransformed in terms of membership. Therefore, its journal is generally and covertly inimical to alternative radical black thought/Afrocentricity. The immediate observations above are based on my experiences, encounters and/or conversations with the editorial offices of the aforementioned journals. Their undeclared ideologies or the covert agendas of their editors and network of reviewers are a disservice to the country's quest to remarkably increase its research output and strengthen the black professoriate (Maserumule, 2015a; Maserumule, 2015b).

Conclusion

Based on document review and interdisciplinary discourse analysis (Maserumule, 2011; Leedy & Ormrod, 2013), this chapter sought to employ Afrocentricity as an alternative lens to critique Sebola's piece *Peer review, scholarship and editors of scientific publications: The death of scientific knowledge in Africa*. It has been established that the subject of the politics of scholarship in Africa, particularly in South Africa, can best be understood when located within a historical and African context. While Sebola's piece provides a partial guide to understanding this discourse, it has been observed that this phenomenon is complex and its unimpressive record can be attributed to several factors, political, socio-economic and technological in nature. While the manner in which some editors and journals handle scientific review leaves much to be desired, the crucial role of scientific peer review and editorship in the production of scholarly knowledge cannot be over-emphasised. It may be necessary for bodies entrusted with monitoring of ethics in the academy to develop and enforce precautionary measures aimed at addressing the isolated cases of flaws in the handling of manuscripts at different production stages, including peer review and editing.

References

Asante, M.K. 2003. *Afrocentricity: The theory of social change*. Chicago: African American Images.

Azibo, D.A. 2011. Understanding essentialism as fundamental: The Centred African Perspective on the Nature of Prototypical Human Nature-Cosmological Ka (Spirit). *The Western Journal of Black Studies*, 35(2), 77-91.

Baylis, J., Smith, S. & Owens, P. (eds). 2008. *The globalization of world politics: An introduction to international relations*. (4th ed.). New York: Oxford University Press.

Carruthers, J.H. 1999. *Intellectual warfare*. Chicago: Third World Press.

Chazan, N. 1988. *Politics and society in contemporary Africa.* Basingstoke: Macmillan.

Earl-Taylor, M. 2018. Ref. The appointment of an External Investigation of the University of Fort Hare: Faculty of Social Sciences and Humanities in 2018: Fraud/Attempted Fraud and Corruption by academic staff in the faculty. A letter written by the former lecturer in the Department of Criminology at the University of Fort Hare to the Honourable Ms N. Pandor, Minister of Higher Education and Training in South Africa.

James, G.G.M. 1954. *Stolen legacy: Greek philosophy was the offspring of the Egyptian mystery system.* New York: E-World.

Katto, J. (2017, December 19). Re: Your submission to NJAS. An email message from the Editorial Assistant of the *Nordic Journal of African Studies* to V.M. Nkuna & the author.

Khalo, T. 2018. Termination of SAAPAM membership. A letter from the SAAPAM national board to Professor M.P. Sebola, 20 June 2018.

Khupe, C. & Keane, M. 2017. Towards an African Education Research Methodology: Decolonising New Knowledge. *Educational Research for Social Change.* 6 (1): 25-37.

Koivu, M. (2017, November 30). VS: Manuscript submission. An email message from the Editorial Office of the *Nordic Journal of African Studies* to V.M. Nkuna and the author.

Koorts, L. (2016, May 07). Re: Manuscript. An email message from *Historia*'s Editor in Chief to the author and T.S. Nyawasha.

Leedy, P.D. & Ormrod, J.E. 2013. *Practical research: Planning and design.* Boston: Pearson.

Manyaka, R.K. 2016. Book review – Local government administration in post-apartheid South Africa: Some critical perspectives, M.P. Sebola (ed.). *Journal of Public Administration, 51*(3):436-441.

Manyaka, R.K. (2017, October 18). RE: Supervision. An email message from a former academic employee of the university in Limpopo to Prof. M.P. Sebola (main supervisor/Director of the School of Economics and Management, university in Limpopo).

Manyaka, R.K. (2017, September 21). FW: Supervision. An email message from a former academic employee of the university in Limpopo to Prof. M.P. Sebola (main supervisor/Director of the School of Economics and Management, university in Limpopo).

Maserumule, M.H. 2011. Good governance in the New Partnership for Africa's Development (NEPAD): A Public Administration perspective. Unpublished PhD Thesis. Pretoria: University of South Africa.

Maserumule, M.H. 2015a. Engaged scholarship and liberatory science: A professoriate, Mount Grace, and SAAPAM in the Decoloniality Mix. *Journal of Public Administration, 50*(2): 200-222.

Maserumule, M.H. 2015b. Why Africa's professors are afraid of colonial education being dismantled. *Mail & Guardian.* http://mg.co.za/articl e/2015-11-26-why-africas-professors-are-afraid-of-colonial-education-being-dismantled (Accessed: 26 November 2015).

Mazama, A. (ed.). 2003. *The Afrocentric paradigm.* Trenton: Africa World Press.

Mekoa, I. 2016. *Silent no more: Challenges facing black African academics at South African universities.* Cape Town: The Incwadi Press.

Muchie, M. & Baskaran, A. (eds). 2013. *Building innovation in Africa: Case studies.* Pretoria: Africa Institute of South Africa.

Nabudere, D.W. 2010. Archie Mafeje: The Scholar and Political Activist – The launching memorial lecture: The Archie Mafeje memorial lecture series. Pretoria: Africa Institute of South Africa.

Ngobeni, S. (ed.). 2010. *Scholarly publishing in Africa: Opportunities and impediments.* Pretoria: Africa Institute of South Africa.

Nkuna, V.M. & Shai, K.B. 2018. An exploration of the 2016 violent protests in Vuwani, Limpopo province of South Africa. *Man in India, 98*(3), 425-436.

Nnadozie, U.O. 2015. Coloniality and governance in Africa in the twenty-first century: The challenges of Public Administration. *Journal of Public Administration, 50*(2), 191-199.

Ray, M. 2016. *Free fall: Why South African universities are in a race against time.* Johannesburg: Bookstorm.

Sebola M.P. 2018. Peer review, scholarship and editors of scientific publications: The death of scientific knowledge in Africa. *KOERS-Bulletin for Christian Scholarship*, 83(1):1-13.

Sesanti, S. (2018, February 14.) *International Journal of African Renaissance Studies* – RARS-2017-0007 has been withdrawn. An email message from the Deputy Editor to the author.

Shai, K.B. 2009. *Rethinking United States-South Africa Relations.* Hoedspruit: Royal B. Foundation.

Shai, K.B. 2012. 'Africa as a threat to the national security of the US: Unpacking claims and realities', in Peace and Security for African

Development, Proceedings of the sixth annual AISA Young Graduates and Scholars (AYGS) Conference, Boksburg, South Africa, 23-26 March 2011.

Shai, K.B. 2016. 'An Afrocentric critique of the United States of America's foreign policy towards Africa: The case studies of Ghana and Tanzania, 1990-2014.' Unpublished PhD Thesis. Sovenga: University of Limpopo.

Shai, K.B. 2017. South African State capture: A symbiotic affair between business and state going bad (?). *Insight on Africa*, 9(1),1-14.

Shai, K.B. 2019a. The death of scientific knowledge in [South] Africa: An Afrocentric response to M.P. Sebola. *Journal of Public Affairs*. e1975. https://doi.org/10.1002/pa.1975

Shai KB. 2019b. [Un] masking Sebola's mythology on the politics of Scholarship in South Africa:

An Afrocentric youth perspective. *Journal of Gender, Information and Development in Africa*. 8 (3): 169-185.

Sithole, M.P. 2009. Unequal Peers. Pretoria: Africa Institute of South Africa.

Tshikwatamba N.E. (2008, October 24). Letter to Dr Sebola in response to several matters.

University of Limpopo. 2018. School of Economics and Management Acting Director: Professor Mokoko Sebola. https://www.ul.ac.za/index.php?Entity=School%20 Main%20 Menu& school_id=5 (Accessed: 20 November 2018).

CHAPTER FOUR

An Afrocentric exploration of the nexus between Sebola's *politricks* of scholarship and [South] Africa's politics of the Doctoral Project

Introduction

The subject of the politics (also read as *politricks*) of scholarship in Africa, especially in South Africa remains under-researched due to several interrelated reasons that are political, socio-economic and technological in nature (Muchie & Baskaran 2013; Mekoa 2016). It is important for the reader to note that this subject has not attracted adequate scholarly attention because there are very few universities (if any) that offer tuition on the politics of scholarship. However, some of the issues pertaining to the subject of the politics of scholarship are treated in passing in publications that emanate from conventional academic disciplines such as Strategic Studies, Sociology, Political Science, Public Administration, International Relations, Information and Publishing Studies, just to mention a few (Shai 2012; Shai 2017). As such, the few scholars who dared to systematically and scientifically research and write about the subject of the politics of scholarship do so on an *ad hoc* basis since they have other primary research interests that are rooted in their respective traditional academic disciplines (Ngobeni 2010; Sithole 2009; Sebola 2018). Of particular importance to note is that most of the few scholars who have entered the discourse on the politics of scholarship have in fact reached the cutting edge of research in their academic disciplines. It is for this reason that a label of activist scholars has stuck on them as opposed to pinned label of anarchist scholars.

However, there appears to be an emerging Eurocentric trend in South Africa led and represented by Mokoko Sebola (2018), who partook in a discourse of judgement without any sound basis, as expressed in his latest article on "the death of scientific knowledge in

Africa" (Tshikwatamba 2008). Coupling the gatekeeping theory (rooted in the Eurocentric world view) and immediate circumstances, the stipulated main argument of Sebola (2018) is that scientific editors and their peer review mechanism and processes are wholly responsible for the self-styled death of scientific knowledge in Africa. He bemoans the allegedly shared unethical conduct between the editors and peer reviewers in the manner in which they conduct their business in respect to the handling of manuscripts. While Sebola's article was published in *KOERS- Bulletin for Christian Scholarship*, Volume 83 (1): 1-13, this journal should not necessarily be a locus of this debate which also raises serious questions about it as it shall be shown later. If published elsewhere, this respose is poised to potentially benefit a wider scholarly community due to its inter-disciplinary nature. Moreover, it is important for Sebola's article to be engaged and corrected (where possible) because of its obvious biases and scholarly deficiencies. Among others, Sebola's article dangerously assumes an African continental posture without zooming the thesis into a test case that would paint a qualitatively rich picture of the phenomena being studied. Sebola also assumes a narrow and simplistic approach to tackling the subject of the politics of scholarship in Africa. It then follows that Sebola's article touched on a sensitive issue of the politics of scholarship in Africa. And everyone interested and deeply invested in the ideational space would be tempted to respond.

While Shai (2019a, 2019b, 2020) has tackled other dimensions of the politics of scholarship in Africa, it is also important for this subject to be expanded and located within the context of the on-going debate about the Doctoral Project in South Africa. Hence, the envisaged success of the Doctoral Project provides a fertile ground for what can be termed the "reincarnation" of scientific knowledge in Africa. Perhaps for reason of context, let me at the outset start by stating the obvious to contextualise my response. I became part of the professoriate with the understanding that this strata of ideation in society derives its essence from the rigour of dialogue, not the shrillness of monologue. And, in this pursuit, there are no holy cows. It is also important to highlight that the Afrocentric epistemic location of this chapter calls for the unveiling of the relevant material facts about the author of the article which is engaged herein. The foregoing observation should be understood within the context that in textual analysis, "once you know the location and time of the researcher or author, it is fairly easy to establish the parameters for the phenom itself" (Asante 2007: 28).

Sebola currently serves as a Professor of Public Administration and Director of the School of Economics and Management at the university in Limpopo (2018). He is also an editor of the *Journal of Public Administration and Development Alternatives (JPADA)*, which is owned and managed by his company called Batalea Publishers (Manyaka 2016a, Manyaka 2016b). Of course, there is nothing wrong with black people owning publication outlets. In fact, this should be encouraged as part of the decoloniality struggle for cognitive justice. However, ownership of publication houses should not be used for self-inscription, instead of contributing to the body of knowledge.

Regardless of the position and status of the author in the knowledge industry, research work riddled with inconsistencies and scholarly weaknesses cannot claim a place in quality research (Rapanyane 2019; Sebola 2019). While Sebola's article, which is the subject of this rejoinder, is riddled with gross factual errors, it is equally concerning that he advances sweeping statements which may not be near the truth if the practical realities of his daily conduct and interaction on the academic landscape is anything to go by (Shai 2019). Emerging from this, Asante (2007: 15) cautions that "there is something more than knowing from an Afrocentric perspective, there is also *doing*".

It is my well-considered view that the observed theoretical and practical contradictions espoused by Sebola can be partly attributed to the fact that over time, he has unknowingly embraced a borrowed epistemological identity (Eurocentricity), which sets him in a serious conflict with his inborn epistemological identity (Afrocentricity) (Azibo 2011; Maserumule 2011). It is for this reason that his article expresses "confused consciousness" which, if left unattended, is likely to cause serious confusions and frustrations for the present and future generation of scholars.

While I reject Sebola's main argument as highlighted above, I argue that by virtue of him being an editor of a journal and selected edited volumes, he might be unintentionally incriminating himself (Manyaka 2016a; Manyaka 2016b; Sebola 2017). The foregoing argument dovetails with Mafeje's (as cited by Nabudere 2010: 16) submission that:

It struck me that in the ensuing social struggles people try to justify themselves and not so much their causes which remain hidden. They do this by authoring particular texts which give them and others certain identities, which in turn become the grammar of the same text, the rules of the game, or if you like, the *modus operandi*, in a social discourse in which individuals by virtue of their ascribed identities are assigned categorical statuses and roles.

Methodological and theoretical framing

Methodologically, I relied on document review, informal conversations and interdisciplinary critical discourse analysis in their broadest form. The location of this chapter within the qualitative realm was informed by my appreciation of its propensity to paint a crispy understanding of a phenomena within the context of a few respondents. Perhaps, it is timely for me to categorically refute any presumptive possibility of this review been misconstrued as a personal attack on Sebola. It is a scholarly conversation with Sebola, who is entitled to respond. For, scholarship cannot be the function of monologue, but dialogue. By its nature, the epistemic location of this chapter is dismissive of the separation of any researcher from his/her views. Also, the empty perceptual space between the researcher and the researched does not find a true and honest expression in the Afrocentric thought system (Maserumule 2011). These principles apply to the current chapter and it is in this spirit that the article under review is approached. The foregoing observation should be understood within the context that "Afrocentrists discard positivist and nomothetic approaches to "reality" as part of their rejection of Eurocentrism" (Milam 1992: 9).

This chapter employs Afrocentricity as its theoretical framework. I consider Afrocentricity as an appropriate theoretical and contextual lens for a chapter of this nature due to its dual cognitive and functional role (Mazama 2003). Equally important, I have opted to underpin this chapter with the Afrocentric theory and paradigm due to its propensity to foster epistemic justice. The latter is achieved by affording Africa-centred ideas, theories and philosophies to co-exist as equals with their North American-Eurocentric counterparts, which were previously and falsely presented as being universally applicable (Shai, 2016). As such, this chapter draws heavily from the works of Asante (2003) and other

Afrocentric scholars. In this context, Stelly (1997) understands "Afrocentricity as a frame of reference wherein phenomena are viewed from the perspective of the African person". Similarly, James (2003: 37) posits that the "Afrocentric approach seeks in every situation the appropriate centrality of the African person". Correspondingly, Asante (2003) defined "Afrocentricity as a paradigm based on the idea that African people should re-assert a sense of agency in order to achieve sanity". An equally significant illustration of Asante (2003) is that an Afrocentric paradigm is a revolutionary shift in thinking proposed as a constructivist adjustment to black disorientation, decenteredness and lack of agency. As a paradigm, Afrocentricity enthrones the centrality of the African. That is, black ideals, motifs, and values as expressed in the highest forms of African culture, and activates consciousness as a functional aspect of any revolutionary approach to phenomena.

Flowing from the above, what makes Afrocentricity the most appropriate lens for engaging with Sebola's thesis is that its focus is on scientific knowledge in Africa. While Afrocentricity does not have a monopoly of utility on this subject, I argue that the use of Eurocentric theories to study African phenomena is prone to the commission of gross substantive transversal errors (Azibo 2011). There is no gainsaying that it is important for the study of scientific knowledge in Africa to be based and centred on historical and lived experiences of the Africans, which is at the very heart of this theoretical framework. Without a doubt, Sebola's melanin confirms that he is an African in terms of biology (Asante 2007) but his positionality on this discourse suggests that he lacks a solid African consciousness, let alone the barest understanding of the decoloniality discourse. Hence, he has subjected himself to Eurocentric etymology, praise mongering of industrialised nations (West) and deliberate or unconscious ignorance of pro-African facts of history. Unlike gatekeeping theory (as used by Sebola) whose usefulness is limited to its cognitive and structural abilities, Afrocentricity extends this to the functional role. It is for this reason that Afrocentricity underpins the research and analysis of this chapter with a view to making the interventions that are necessary for advancing the interests of Africans and Africa.

Some salient points and the doctoral project in South Africa

Recent studies reveal that Africa does not contribute more than 2% of the global scientific knowledge (Sebola 2018). It is for this reason that the South African government has a flagship doctoral project led by, among others, National Research Foundation (NRF), National Institute of Humanities and Social Sciences (NIHSS) and Young Southern African Scholars Program (YSSP) (Gumede 2019). The latter is a joint initiative of the NRF and the Vienna, Austria-based International Institute of Applied Systems Analysis (IIASA). These are some of the great interventions by the government in South Africa in partnership with other governments in Africa and beyond, which are meant to improve on what is sadly painted by Sebola (2018) as the death of scientific knowledge. Sebola provocatively cries foul that "gatekeeping" as practised by editors and peer reviewers is at the centre of retarded scientific knowledge production in Africa. On gatekeeping, the article suggests rather unconvincingly that editors somehow self-servingly reject certain articles for no particular reason but to safeguard the reputations of their journals. This is a bad claim and it amounts to bad reasoning. If it is anything to go by, it possibly represents an oasis in the ocean of the poverty of Africa's knowledge industry. The author seems to confuse the word scholarship with peer-review. Moreover, the author does not seem to comprehend what peer review is meant to achieve. And he also fails to appreciate that peer review is not necessarily an end in itself. We have post-publication peer review and peer review reports can be easily contested.

I also refuse to agree with Sebola that Africa's 2% contribution to global scientific knowledge fits the description of "death" as embedded in the title of his article. Philosophically and etymologically, his description is in total conflict with the African notion of "deathlessness" which adequately captures the essence of the reappearance of ancestors (Asante 2007: 26). Perhaps, this salient point reflects the extent to which the title of Sebola's article is badly formulated. An article's title should encapsulate its thesis. This one is all over the show. Reading it, I am not sure of what the author intended to do. It also speaks volumes about the 'editor' of the journal, let alone the people they use for copy editing and proofreading. In the past millennium, this 2% contribution to global scientific knowledge has not been any higher. In fact, the current percentage is quite a progressive shift compared to the colonial era. As expressed in the National Development Plan (NDP), the South African government's belief is that if the production of doctoral graduates in South Africa and Africa at large can be remarkably increased, the country and continent would be well poised to make meaningful contributions to global scientific knowledge (National Planning Commission 2012). With such clearly co-ordinated efforts to build the scholarly cadre-ship of tomorrow, the enhancement of the current contribution of Africa to global scientific knowledge is not in doubt.

The pessimistic views of scholars such as Sebola on this matter are not near the truth and may be a reflection of the frustration by the old and unprogressive professoriate who cannot keep up with the dynamism of the knowledge industry in Africa (Maserumule 2015a; Ray 2016). It is common knowledge that some senior academics ride on networking and emotional attachment to get their work published (Mekoa, 2018). When their articles are rejected in certain journals, they then resort to casting aspersions on the whole credibility of such editors and their peer review mechanisms and processes. This situation becomes worse especially if the affected journals are perceived to be giving preferential treatment in publishing the work of competent young scholars as opposed to incompetent but well-positioned senior scholars. Related to this, a simple inter-generational lesson in academic writing is that an incisive abstract should contain aim, method, results, conclusions and recommendations. Unfortunately, the abstract of the article under review may not pass this test. Frankly, it is bad. The aim of the article, which is propounded in the introduction, is also not in line with the title. The title of a paper and the aim should be on a tangent. You cannot state that the study seeks to examine the efficacy of the peer review process as well as editors' efficacy in knowledge generation and then title it 'PEER REVIEW, SCHOLARSHIP AND EDITORS OF SCIENTIFIC PUBLICATIONS : THE DEATH OF SCIENTIFIC KNOWLEDGE IN AFRICA'. The two are not speaking to each other. These are elementary shortcomings of an article written by a senior scholar and the totality of this serves as a very good example of bad articles or articles that should not be published.

The professorial old guard are so used to dominating the closed intellectual space to a point wherein entrance by new and young scholars is deemed to be a threat to the status quo (Maserumule 2015b; Gumede 2019). Relatedly, I am reminded of a young scholar at the university in Limpopo whose application for promotion to Associate Professor was declined in 2019 without any sound basis. For this rank, the policy requirement of the university in question was 5 Department of Higher Education and Training (DHET)-recognised publications. The applicant had 6 DHET-recognised publications; which implies that he superseded the established requirements. But his application was declined because he did not have sufficient Masters students' supervision record and most of his publications were recent. Inasmuch as the applicant only had one Masters graduate, the academic promotion policy at this university was silent on postgraduate supervision record in quantitative terms. More so, the promotion policy did not state anything about the age of the publications that are fit for their producer to be considered for promotion. That such a negative feedback was never provided in writing to the applicant may be a trick used by those in power to cover up inconsistency and lack of transparency in the manner in which applications for promotion are adjudicated. Perhaps I should hasten to point out, in this example, that the problem at the said university is not its policy on promotion, but people who interpret the policy to suit their whims.

Considering that postgraduate supervision is a form of research output, weakness on this aspect could easily be compensated by publications (which are research outputs in their own right). The latter can be a consideration wherein social justice reigns rather than corporatisation and empty egos of the academic managerial class. Lewis Gordon (as cited in Ndlovu-Gatsheni, 2017: 73) aptly views this class as "consisting of failed academics and scholars" who practise the "sociology of revenge and entrenched resentment toward productive and influential scholars". The university in Limpopo does not have a monopoly of toxic sociology when it comes to the need for rewarding meritocracy when it comes to recruitment, retention and promotion of academics at the professoriate level and beyond. Perhaps, this is reflective of the depth of the general moral decay in the South African society.

The intellectual space in Africa was previously dominated and manipulated by old and white males (and a few Blacks in their circle) to serve a particular political and economic cause (Shai 2009). The foregoing observation is well captured by Nabudere (2010: 1) when he avers that "the British were initially not concerned principally with military or economic power over Egypt, but their knowledge of the Orients, including Egypt, was conceived as a form of power". Now that there are fundamental changes at the political and academic level to a point wherein serious Black scholars in Africa are also afforded the rare opportunity to serve as editors of credible scientific publications (i.e. *Journal of Public Administration [JOPA], Strategic Review for Southern Africa [SRSA]* and etc), a new tendency can be observed that the old and conservative white professoriate in South Africa possibly rent pockets of Black academics to peddle unscientific views which does nothing except to undermine Black academic excellence and progress ("Minutes" 2010; Nnadozie 2015; Nkuna & Shai 2018). This analysis does not suggest that Sebola is a rented academic. It simply highlights that his views as captured in the article under review are questionable and warrants deep reflection by all academics.

Among others, the underhanded and unprogressive mechanisations hinted above have produced unintended consequences in the form of hardened attitudes between local and African expatriate academics. In relation to this, Carruthers (1999: 156) cautions that "many observers believe that South Africa would be free of white supremacy immediately if only the Africans would stop fighting among themselves, and adopt a unified stance". Emerging from this caution, my response to Sebola's article should not be construed in any way as an expression of Black on Black scholarly attack. This response is inspired by two premises. As it is the case in common law, self-defence is justifiable in this context because Sebola's article is apparently casting unwarranted aspersions on Black scientific editors and scholarly publications produced in Africa. While his article is located within the global, continental and regional context, it is clear that his real qualms are with the management and administration of *JOPA*. Considering that Sebola became a Professor largely through publications that appeared in *JOPA* and until very recently, he served as a member of the National Board of Directors of the SAAPAM, his recent reservations about *JOPA* are questionable (Sebola 2012; Nkuna &

Sebola 2012; Manyaka & Sebola 2012). In this case and without any anecdotes of evidence, Sebola (2018:3) says "that his [Maserumule] experience in the editorial chair of the same journal opposed his polemic editorial to justify that editorial "gatekeeping is the only solution to keep the integrity of scholarship of the Journal of Public Administration". In the absence of such much-needed evidence, the author's interpretation cannot stand and equally, his approach to the problem would be vulnerable to poor conclusions (Asante 2007).

Sebola's inconsistency in the intellectual interpretation and processing of issues that matter to the academic landscape of Africa and South Africa in particular is not new. For example, Sebola holds a Doctor of Technology (D. Tech) degree from Tshwane University of Technology (TUT), which is more or less the same as the Doctor of Philosophy (PhD) offered in traditional universities at level 10 of the South African National Qualifications Framework (NQF) (South African Qualifications Authority [SAQA] 2010). Ironically, those who have been close to Sebola in one way or the other at some point in time would tell you that it is not uncommon for him to refer to TUT as a glorified high school which is meant for intellectually weak students who could not competently pass the matric. His invocation in this regard is far from the truth. It is also an act of self-invalidation because he is currently serving at the traditional university in Limpopo on the basis of his terminal qualification from TUT (Tshikwatamba 2008). But then, Tshikwamba's (2008) analysis of the person, character and stature of Sebola vindicates my conviction that Sebola is not new to a tendency to praise certain individuals and institutions when it is convenient for him or when it well serves his narrow personal and political agenda. He is equally capable of demonising those individuals and institutions who disagree with his opinions. The foregoing analysis accounts for the "powder keg" for Sebola's self-centredness and selfishness on the academic landscape, which embarrassingly finds expression at times in his scholarly writing as is the case in the article under review.

Perhaps, Sebola's frustration on the point of divergence and convergence between D. Tech and PhD best explains the recent Doctor of Commerce (D. Com) scandal at the university in Limpopo, which was reported by the media as involving a senior university official who was enrolled in a school that is led and directed by Sebola (Ramothwala 2018). There is no gainsaying that the recent D. Com saga at the university in Limpopo happened under the full watch of Sebola in his capacity as the Acting Director of the School of the Economics and Management at the same university (University of Limpopo, 2018). The failure of Sebola to enforce established institutional monitoring and evaluation tools resulted in his school's failure to ensure that only qualifying students are admitted into its doctoral programs and they at least spend the minimum duration for the qualifications before the degree can be awarded. This major weakness has resulted in the university in Limpopo facing litigation by some of the affected students and also in the good name of this glorious institution of higher learning being brought into disrepute. It remains to be seen whether the university in Limpopo would institute disciplinary measures against Sebola and other implicated parties as a deterrence for the recurrence of inconsistent interpretation and application of admission rules. It is my invocation that such theoretical and practical tendencies on the part of Sebola do nothing except to undo the good work of the government's doctoral project and its long term goal of enhancing South Africa and Africa's contribution to global scientific knowledge. It is also painstaking that the university in Limpopo does not have a monopoly on scandals that have to do with the aborted awarding of doctoral degrees at a university (Ledwaba 2018). However, it is encouraging that at the university in Limpopo some of the questionable doctoral degrees have been withheld and some of the parties involved have been permanently released from their duties (BEMAWU 2018). Despite this, one wonders how many fraudulently doctoral degrees have been awarded at the university in Limpopo and beyond at least before 2018 when this syndicate was disrupted. These are some of the factors that lend credence to calls in certain quarters for doctoral qualifications offered by universities in South Africa to be reviewed (Council on Higher Education 2018; McKenna 2019).

Flowing from the above, I am reminded of the English adage that "if you live in a glass house do not throw stones". The essence of this adage is derived from an observation that was once echoed by one young academic A in reference to a fellow young academic B: "Promoted and mentored by a historian and psychologist is equals to identity crisis". The basis for this observation is the fact that the PhD (International Politics) for academic B was supervised by a historian and co-supervised by a psychologist who is an NRF-rated researcher. Academically, there is nothing wrong about a combination of this nature when it comes to a postgraduate student's supervision team. This is because in International Politics, we consider History as our laboratory (Shai 2016). As such, entrusting a historian with the responsibility of overseeing the substantive issues relating to the operationalisation of a study in International Politics is not misplaced by any sensible academic standard (Shai, Molapo & Sodi 2017). Besides the fact that the discipline also draws its expertise from Psychology (Baylis, Smith & Owens 2008), the involvement of a psychologist as a co-supervisor of the doctoral study of academic B was largely influenced by the fact that the psychologist in question is an academic guru in Afrocentric theory and paradigm. But it is not surprising that such a misguided and anarchic observation comes from academic A who happens to be in the same circle with Sebola and his PhD (Public Administration) is supervised by a senior scholar (Sebola) whose writing in the article under review and beyond suggests that he might be intellectually frustrated. This observation is shared by Tshikwatamba (2008) who avers that:

> A Public Administration student who did the discipline from first level, to second level up to third level may have a more advanced knowledge of the field of Public Administration than Dr Sebola has acquired in his academic journey, thus depriving our students in the deployment of Dr Sebola in the Department of Public Administration.

It may not be too far-fetched to believe that academic A has learned and imbedded such ill-informed provincialisation and colonisation of academic disciplines from Sebola (Ndlovu-Gatsheni 2018). Hence, Sebola is not well-grounded in Public Administration, a field which he only studied at the doctoral level. His academic orientation is mainly in Educational Studies and Tourism Management (Tshikwatamba 2008). It is instructive for the reader to also note that his Master's degree (Development Planning and Management) was supervised by NRF rated geographer at the university in Limpopo. There is no doubt that the latter is a serious scholar of Geography.

What is concerning is that Sebola finds comfort in being supervised by scholars outside his newly found academic discipline, yet he has qualms when the same is extended to other emerging scholars. He is not consistent in this regard. He also fails to appreciate that such circumstances are often dictated by poor post-graduate supervision capacity in certain academic departments of particular universities, more especially previously disadvantaged universities such as the universities in Limpopo and other rural provinces. The state of post-graduate supervision capacity in previously disadvantaged universities' academic disciplines such as History and Political Science cannot be delinked from the far-reaching legacy and impact of apartheid. Undoing such a painful legacy cannot be a once-off event and it requires well-targeted goals and shared vision among all South African academics (Hall 2007).

In 2017, Sebola shared with me (in confidence) that the Quality Assurance (QA) unit at the university in Limpopo had previously registered baseless concerns about the involvement of a historian and psychologist in the supervision of academic B's doctoral thesis in International Politics. The foregoing analysis is a clear demonstration that the manipulated intellectual orientation of the Sebolas partly contributes to retarded scientific knowledge in Africa. Having said this, it is timely for me to briefly advance lessons that the cross-pollination of scholarly ideas that Sebola rejects or accepts willy-nilly finds true and honest expression in inter-disciplinarity. As correctly pointed out and contextualised by the editor of *Historia*, interdisciplinary works are "those that conform to the approach and methodology of historical studies, but which draw on the insights offered by theoretical frameworks and methodologies from other disciplines to enhance their findings" (Koorts 2016). In recognition of the dangerous tapestry of inward looking, societal problems of today equally demands an inter-disciplinary approach because they are complex in nature and orientation.

Conclusion

Based on document review and interdisciplinary critical discourse analysis, this chapter sought to employ Afrocentricity as an alternative contextual lens to tease out the major contradictions espoused in Sebola's contribution to the discourse on the politics of scholarship in Africa, particularly in South Africa. It has been observed that while Africa's contribution to global scientific knowledge may not be impressive in the eyes of others, the description of its state as "death" constitutes an over-exaggeration. Using the South African doctoral project as a test case has painted a picture that shows that the attribution of the dire state of scientific knowledge in Africa to editors of scholarly publications fails to acknowledge the strategic and tactical role that post-graduate studies have on the preparation of the next generation of serious thought leaders who ought to be intellectually sharpened today in preparation of pushing the frontiers of knowledge in the proverbial tomorrow. While the development and growth of scientific knowledge in [South] Africa may not be pleasing in quantitative terms, it is worth acknowledging that the problem is complex. It cannot be reduced to a linear, quick, cheap and simplistic analysis as presented in the article under review. In the final analysis, I conclude that some of the theoretical and practical contradictions evident in Sebola's discourse cannot be delinked from his extreme intellectual frustration, which emanates from his unconscious or rather uncritical embracing of an alien epistemological identity rooted in the North American and Eurocentric worldview. Otherwise, the rest of his article does not make any meaningful contribution to knowledge. Journal articles are supposed to push the frontiers of knowledge. They are meant to 'open our eyes to a world we only thought we knew'.[2] Unfortunately, same cannot be said of this article. It offers nothing new. Lastly, the copy editing as well as proofreading of the journal that published Sebola's article leaves a lot to be desired! The editing and proofreading were very sloppy, hence the prevalence of badly constructed sentences and simply bad syntax.

References

Academic A (*real name was withheld on ethical grounds). (2018, August 08). "Promoted and mentored by a historian and psychologist is equals to identity crisis", Facebook Status Update.

Asante M.K. 2003. Afrocentricity: *The Theory of Social Change*. Chicago: African American Images.

Asante M.K. 2007. *An Afrocentric Manifesto*. Cambridge: Polity Press.

---

[2] This observation is drawn from my electronic conversation (dated 7 January 2020) with Solani Ngobeni, who is a well renowned publisher in South Africa.

Azibo D.A. 2011. Understanding Essentialism as Fundamental: The Centred African Perspective on the Nature of Prototypical Human Nature- Cosmological Ka (Spirit). *The Western Journal of Black Studies*, Vol 35 (2): 77-91.

Baylis J., Smith S. & Owens P (eds). 2008. The *Globalization of World Politics: An Introduction to International Relations*. (4th Ed). New York: Oxford University Press.

Broadcasting, Electronic, Media & Allied Workers Union (BEMAWU). 2018. Court intervened in Doctorate of SABC Board Member | BEMAWU. http://bemawu.org.za/2018/04/18/court-intervened-doctorate-sabc-board-member-bemawu/ (accessed 18 April 2018).

Carruthers J.H. 1999. *Intellectual Warfare*. Chicago: Third World Press.

Council on Higher Education (CHE). 2018. CHE Launches National Reviews of Doctoral Studies. www.che.ac.za (accessed 25 December 2018).

Gumede V. 2019. Is there a doctor in the house? We need more PhD graduates. *Daily Maverick*. https://www.dailymaverick.co.za/opinionista/2019-11-13-is-there-a-doctor-in-the-house-we-need-more-phd-graduates/ (Accessed 13 November 2019)

Hall M. 2007. Transformation and Continuity in the University in Africa. *Social Dynamics*. Vol 33 (01): 181-198.

James C. 2003. *Afrocentricity and the academy: Essay on theory and practise*. Unknown City: McFarland.

Koorts L. (2016, May 07). Re: Manuscript. An email message from *Historia*'s Editor in Chief to academic B and C (authors)*.

Ledwaba K. 2018. Professor killed over fraudulent PhDs. *Sowetan*.

Manyaka R.K. & Sebola, M.P. 2012. Impact of performance management on service delivery in the South African public service. *Journal of Public Administration*, Vol 47 (Special issue 1): 299-310.

Manyaka R.K. 2016a. Book Review- Local Government Administration in Post-Apartheid South Africa: Some Critical Perspectives, MP Sebola (Ed.). *Journal of Public Administration*, Vol 51 (3): 436-441.

Manyaka R.K. (2016b, October 18). RE: Supervision. An email message from a former academic employee of the University of Limpopo to Prof MP Sebola (main supervisor/ Acting Director of the School of Economics and Management, University of Limpopo).

Manyaka R.K. (2017, September 21). FW: Supervision. An email message from a former academic employee of the University of Limpopo to Prof MP Sebola (main supervisor/ Director of the School of Economics and Management, University of Limpopo).

Maserumule M.H. 2011. Good Governance in the New Partnership for Africa's Development (NEPAD: A Public Administration Perspective. Unpublished PhD Thesis. Pretoria: University of South Africa.

Maserumule M.H. 2015a. Engaged Scholarship and Liberatory Science: A Professoriate, Mount Grace, and SAAPAM in the Decoloniality Mix. *Journal of Public Administration*, Vol 50 (2): 200-222.

Maserumule M.H. 2015b. Why Africa's professors are afraid of colonial education being dismantled. *Mail & Guardian*, http://mg.co.za/articl e/2015-11-26-why-africas-professors-are-afraid-of-colonial-education-being-dismantled (Accessed 26 November 2015).

Mazama A. (Ed). 2003. *The Afrocentric Paradigm*. Trenton: Africa World Press.

McKenna S. 2019. South Africa takes steps to assure the quality of its doctorates. *The Conversation.* https://theconversation.com/south-africa-takes-steps-to-assure-the-q bruality-of-its-doctorates-125774 (Accessed 06 November 2019).

Mekoa I. 2016. *Silent No More: Challenges Facing Black African Academics at South African Universities*. Cape Town: The Incwadi Press.

Mekoa I. 2018. *The Battle for the Soul of South African Universities: Institutional Cultures, Racism and Ideologies*. Cape Town: Incwadi Press.

Milam, J.H., Jr. 1992. "The Emerging Paradigm of Afrocentric Research Methods"., Paper presented at the 17th Annual Meeting of the Association for the Study of Higher Education in Minneapolis, Minnesota, 30 October 1992.

Minutes of an Extraordinary General Meeting of Members of the South African Association of Public Administration and Management (SAAPAM) held at Villa Sterne, Pretoria, (2010, August 27).

Muchie M. & Baskaran A. (Eds) 2013. *Building Innovation in Africa: Case Studies*. Pretoria: Africa Institute of South Africa.

Nabudere D.W. 2010. *Archie Mafeje: The Scholar and Political Activist* – The launching memorial lecture: The Archie Mafeje memorial lecture series. Pretoria: Africa Institute of South Africa.

National Planning Commission. 2012. *National Development Plan 2030: Our Future- make it work.* Pretoria: National Planning Commission.

Ndlovu-Gatsheni S.J. 2017. The Emergence and Trajectories of Struggles for an 'African University': The Case of Unfinished Business of African Epistemic Decolonisation. *Kronos,* Vol 43 (1): 51-77.

Ndlovu-Gatsheni S.J. 2018. *Epistemic Freedom in Africa: Deprovincialization and Decolonization.* London: Routledge.

Ngobeni S. (Ed) (2010. *Scholarly Publishing in Africa: Opportunities and Impediments.* Pretoria: Africa Institute of South Africa.

Nkuna N.W. & Sebola M.P. 2012. Public administration theoretical discourse in South Africa and the developmental local government: A need to go beyond modern thinking. *Journal of Public Administration,* Vol 47 (Special issue 1): 68-87.

Nkuna V.M. & Shai K.B. 2018. An exploration of the 2016 violent protests in Vuwani, Limpopo province of South Africa. *Man in India,* Vol 98 (3): 425-436.

Nnadozie U.O. 2015. Coloniality and Governance in Africa in the Twenty-First Century: The Challenges of Public Administration. *Journal of Public Administration,* Vol 50 (2): 191-199.

Ramothwala P. 2018. University of Limpopo spokesperson put on leave over qualification. *Sowetan.* https://www.sowetanlive.co.za/news/south-africa/2018-06-07-university-of-limpopo-spokesperson-put-on-leave-over-qualification/ (Accessed 07 June 2018).

Rapanyane MB. 2019. Book Review: Mokoko P Sebola (ed) Local Government: Elections, Politics and Administration. *Strategic Review for Southern Africa.* Vol 41 (01): 124-128.

Ray M. 2016. *Free Fall: Why South African Universities are in a Race Against Time.* Johannesburg: Bookstorm.

Sebola M.P. 2012. Objective role of the South African media industry: The watchdogs for good governance and service delivery. *Journal of Public Administration,* Vol 47 (Special issue 1): 407-419.

Sebola M.P. (Ed.) 2017. *Local Government Elections, Politics & Administration.* Polokwane: Batalea Publishers.

Sebola M.P. 2018. Peer review, scholarship and editors of scientific publications: the death of scientific knowledge in Africa. *KOERS-Bulletin for Christian Scholarship,* Vol 83 (1):1-13.

Sebola M.P. 2019. Governance and Student Leadership in South African Universities: Co-Governing with Those to Be Governed. *Journal of Gender, Information and Development in Africa*. Vol 8 (2): 7-18.

Shai K.B. 2009. *Rethinking United States-South Africa Relations*. Hoedspruit: Royal B. Foundation.

Shai K.B. 2012. "Africa as a threat to the national security of the US: Unpacking claims and realities", in *Peace and Security for African Development*, Proceedings of the sixth annual AISA Young Graduates and Scholars (AYGS) Conference, Boksburg, South Africa, 23-26 March 2011.

Shai K.B. 2016. An Afrocentric Critique of the United States of America's foreign policy towards Africa: The case studies of Ghana and Tanzania, 1990-2014. Unpublished PhD Thesis. Sovenga: University of Limpopo.

Shai K.B. 2017. South African State Capture: A Symbiotic Affair between Business and State Going Bad (?). *Insight on Africa*, Vol 9 (1): 1-14.

Shai K.B, Molapo R.R. & Sodi T. 2017. The United States of America's post-1990 foreign policy towards West Africa: The case study of Ghana. *Journal for Contemporary History*, Vol 42 (1): 154-173.

Shai K.B. 2019. The death of scientific knowledge in [South] Africa: An Afrocentric response to M.P. Sebola. *Journal of Public Affairs*. e1975. https://doi.org/10.1002/pa.1975

Shai K.B. 2019. [Un]masking Sebola's Mythology on the Politics of Scholarship in South Africa: An Afrocentric Youth Perspective. *Journal of Gender, Information and Development in Africa*, Vol 8 (3): 169-185.

Shai K.B. 2020. Mokoko Sebola on 'Scientific Knowledge in Africa': An Afrocentric Critique. *African Renaissance*, Vol 17 (1): 143-156

Sithole M.P. 2009. *Unequal Peers*. Pretoria: Africa Institute of South Africa.

South African Qualifications Authority (SAQA). 2010. Level Descriptors for the South African National Qualifications Framework. Pretoria: SAQA.

Stelly M. 1997. Afrocentrism as an intellectual tool of whites: a critique of Molefi Asante. Different perspectives on majority rules. Digitalcommons.un (Accessed 05 May 2018).

Tshikwatamba N.E. (2008, October 24). Letter to Dr Sebola in response to several matters.

University of Limpopo. 2018. School of Economics and Management Acting Director: Professor Mokoko Sebola. https://www.ul.ac.za/index.php?Entity=School%20Main%20Menu&school_id=5 (Accessed 20 November 2018).

CHAPTER FIVE

Decay of scientific knowledge industry in Africa: An Afrocentric pre-parting shot

Introduction

The subject of scientific knowledge is complex and in Africa in particular, it is not uniformly understood. The competing explanations about the state of scientific knowledge in Africa can be attributed to the fact that its politics are characterised by higher stakes between individuals, nation states, regions and continents (Mekoa, 2016). While explanations about scientific knowledge in Africa are diverse, the dominant narrative is the outcry about the seemingly little contribution of resident Africans (also referred as Africans of the soil by Ali Mazrui) to the knowledge structure of the global political economy (Shai & Mothibi, 2015; Sebola, 2018). Roughly forty years since the demise of colonialism in Africa, the insistence on historical imperatives such as imperialism, colonialism and apartheid as still responsible for the dearth of scientific knowledge in Africa is fast becoming unfashionable. The relevance of historical imperatives in this discourse is debatable (Nnadozie, 2015). I argue that inasmuch as history possess useful lessons for the present, it should not be [ab]used to overlook the contribution of the immediate dynamics. This calls for sober analysis that equitably appreciates the past and present factors influencing the state of scientific knowledge in Africa. This subject has been significantly debated in Africa and the Diaspora. But there has been little improvement largely because the knowledge structure cannot be divorced from economic and trade structures of the global political economy (Shai, 2017). This implies that the stubborn and unfair rules governing international trade do not provide an enabling environment wherein Africans can make a meaningful contribution to scientific knowledge. The poor performance of most economies in Africa makes it difficult for African states to invest on the necessary intellectual infrastructure; yet the latter is equally important for economic growth and development (Mekoa, 2018).

This reflection is important because the voices of young academics are often un-heard in respect of their plight in the knowledge industry (Shai, 2019b). What also elevates the status of the focus of this chapter is that it transcends all academic disciplines. While the extent to which the dictum of "publish or perish" has impacted the livelihood of young academics is well accounted in literature, not enough work has been done to explore the external human impediments to their academic growth (Lee, 2014). Due to fears of victimisation, most young academics do not openly voice the unfair and un-transparent nature of the treatment that they are often subjected to by their seniors in their academic journey. This is especially worse in Africa where it is common to find strong men and women leaders instead of strong institutions and systems (Louw-Vaudran, 2013). An exceptional case among a few courageous young academics wrote the following to his non-immediate line manager on the 1st August 2019:

> Let me begin by apologising for writing directly to you. I am fully aware that your preferred approach in regard to matters of this nature is that they should be communicated through your secretary. But then, writing to you has been a painful exercise that I had to 'deeply' think about for over 2 full weeks. Having said this, I am writing to you today for the purpose of requesting a meeting with you at a date and time convenient to your kind self. If you are agreeable, I would appreciate that my immediate line manager joins us in the proposed meeting. The purpose of the proposed meeting is to have a collegial engagement with you regarding what appears to be the "unfair" manner in which you personally treat submissions (i.e. applications for leave of absence) from me. As the Head of the faculty where I am administratively based, I think you are well positioned to clear the dampened prevailing working conditions that negatively impact my productivity.

Whether the note above served its purpose is beyond the scope of this chapter. A key lesson to be drawn from the extracted note above is the deficit of *Ubuntu/botho* in the professional working relations between some senior executives and their subordinates.

Given the large size of Africa, this chapter employs South Africa as a test case to paint a qualitatively rich picture of the state of scientific knowledge within a limited context (Platt, 2007). The logic behind the use of Afrocentricity as the theoretical and contextual microscope in studying the subject of this chapter cannot be over-emphasised as this aspect has been extensively covered by Shai (2019a, 2019b, 2020a, 2020b) and to a certain extent Asante (1990, 2003). What follows below is the exploration of some of the notable issues that cause the dearth of scientific knowledge in South Africa and to a larger extent, Africa. Given the many commonalities between South Africa and other states in Africa and the global South, it is envisaged that lessons emerging from the research of this chapter will benefit a wider segment of the developing world (Chazan, 1988).

Theory and methods

This chapter is foregrounded by Afrocentric theory (also read as Afrocentricity) as propagated by Asante (2003). It also draws from the works of other Afrocentric scholars such as Modupe (2003) and Legodi (2019), *inter alia*. Modupe (2003) identified grounding, orientation and perspective as the tenets of Afrocentricity; which are in turn operationalised as the analytical categories of this chapter. Afrocentricity asserts that when Africans view themselves as central in their own history, they see themselves as agents, actors, and participants rather than as marginal and on the periphery of political and socio-economic experiences. The choice of Afrocentricity as the contextual and theoretical lens of this chapter was informed by its underlying desire to *unmute* genuine African voices on discourses about higher education and scholarship in Africa and South Africa in particular (Maleka & Shai, 2016). While the utility of North[ern] angled theories (i.e. ethics theory) in the study of higher education and scholarship cannot be disputed, it is argued that a study based on Afrocentricity will potentially paint an alternative and qualitatively rich picture of the phenomena being studied. Asante (2003) lends credence to the foregoing by asserting that there is absolutely nothing that our Afrocentricity cannot explain. For him (Asante, 2020), Afrocentricity can stand on its own and it does not need the help or support of alien theories to capture the essence of African reality. The choice and use of South Africa as a test case for this chapter was informed by the propensity of case study designs to generate a crispy understanding of a phenomena being studied in a context of limited participants (Shai, 2016). To add, the Afrocentric epistemic location of this chapter is dismissive of the binary standing of knowledge as either empirical/non-empirical, good/evil, qualitative/quantitative and etc (Maserumule, 2011; Shai & Nyawasha, 2016). In this spirit, the empty perceptual space between the researcher and the researched is non-existent. Such space is rejected as a cheap and false façade of Western scholarship.

Emerging from the above, it goes without saying that this chapter touches on critical issues that are currently of interest for those working in the field of ethics in higher education and governance in universities in Africa as well as bringing attention to a relatively new case study – the Afrocentric as against the Eurocentric perspective in knowledge production. Although of current interest, and despite obsolete power relationships within academia borne out of selfish cronyism that stifles intellectual dynamism this subject is emphatically under researched. The selfishness tendencies laid bare in this chapter are a by-product of Eurocentric value system (Shai, Nyawasha & Ndaguba, 2018). Hence, they potentially possess a dangerous recipe for sabotaging the prolific production of African scholarship in the direction of scientific knowledge. To this end, Ubuntu/ *botho*/ humanness is a pillar of the Afrocentric value system which is equally critical to understanding the strained relationship between the academic narrative of frustration, bigotry and inconsistency in South Africa's higher education sector. Far from the Eurocentric value system's embodiments of individualism, selfishness and competition; this chapter openly embraces oneness, cooperation, interdependence and collaboration as the anchors of the Afrocentric value system which ought to define the higher education sector of South Africa and Africa as a whole. The latter is a non-negotiable pre-condition for improved higher education and scientific knowledge in Africa. This submission may be debatable because of the lack of uniform conception of ethics in the society. Despite this, I argue that as Africans we have points of convergence in terms of what is good or bad. For example, all religions in Africa (and elsewhere) condemns violence.

Tricks for academic stagnation in Limpopo

In South African universities, the path to academic promotion is presented at a distance as a reward for excellence in either research and/or teaching (Higher Education Transformation Network, 2020). But a closer look reveals that this path is not smooth sailing as it appears. Depending on one's proximity to the academic managerial class, the road to academic heights promotion or professorship can either be a rough texture or a bed of roses (Ndlovu-Gatsheni, 2017). A clear case of a rough ride can be witnessed in the case of young academic X at a certain university in Limpopo.[3] He filed an application for promotion from Associate Professor to Full Professor on the 16th August 2019. Despite written and oral representations, his line manager has declined to process his application. This is because at the time of filing the application, he had "not as yet supervised a PhD [Doctor of Philosophy) candidate to completion".[4] But this criterion is not a mandatory requirement in terms of the approved academic promotion policy at the university in question. Precedence was also laid during the cycle of the enforcement of the approved policy on academic promotion. For example, several cases of academics without a traceable record of "completed" PhD supervision who have been promoted to full professorship at the same university in Limpopo are also evident. As such, the decision of the line manager in question not to process young academic X's application is arbitrary, unfair and inconsistent by any measurable standards. Apparently, the line manager is fully aware of this. But he does not wish to find himself in conflict with his seniors, who introduced the "completed PhD supervision" rule willy-nilly and without the backing of the approved academic promotion policy. The reader should note that arbitrary decisions to block the rise of some individuals in academy are not necessarily the official position of the institutions where such practices manifest. It can either be personal or collective decisions of the dominant faction within management circles at a particular level. It is for

---

[3] South Africa's Limpopo Province is blessed with four universities, namely: University of Limpopo, University of Venda, University of South Africa and Tshwane University of Technology. The latter two are in fact, satellite campuses of universities that are headquartered in the City of Tshwane, Gauteng.

[4] I cite the words of the line manager here verbatim.

this reason that while applications for promotion are made in writing, negative feedback is always withheld and when it is really demanded by the applicant that is when it is furnished verbally. The strategy by the bearers of concocted bad news is to avoid taking responsibility by communicating written feedback that cannot be easily defended in platforms that are mediated by external bodies such as the *Commission for Conciliation, Mediation and Arbitration* (CCMA) and Labour Court (CCMA, 2020). Such treacherous individual or shared missions are not driven by the desire to better the lives of those who are led or the institution as a whole. The ideology behind them is simply to entrench personal greed. This posture is reminiscent of members of the academic managerial class who have a shallow conception of the essence of leadership in a dynamic institution such as a university (Ndlovu-Gatsheni, 2017).

At the time of writing this chapter, there was a process to incorporate "completed doctoral supervision" as criterion for promotion to Full Professorship at the same University I have referred to earlier. However, it is procedurally improper for a draft policy to be used at certain levels to assess the readiness of certain academics to be considered for professorial promotion. To compound matters to an already worst situation, the foregoing narrative is not the first experience of academic X to be blocked without any sound basis as and when he applied for promotion. His application from Senior Lecturer to Associate Professor was previously held in abeyance for over a year simply because of reasons which could not stand the must of institutional policy and the country's labour relations framework (Shai, 2020a). At least, the Associate Professorship was ultimately awarded in April 2019 following the successful appeal/ intervention by the local branch of National Education, Health and Allied Workers Union (NEHAWU). I am afraid that if labour unions do not timeously and consistently challenge arbitrary decisions of this nature, unfair and inconsistent academic promotion practices will become the norm in South African universities and elsewhere. The sad part is that in cases where appeals are successful, monetary reward is not backdated and this was exactly the case when young academic X was promoted to Associate Professorship. The fact that such inconsistencies in the handling of academic promotion happen under the full watch of internal and external auditors is puzzling and leaving one to question their envisaged role in fostering and advancing accountability in public institutions such as universities. If the compromised position of the KPMG official(s) in the recent VBS great bank heist is anything to go by, then the possibility of underhand tactics to 'panel-beat' adverse audit findings in Human Resources (HR) processes at some universities in South Africa cannot be ruled out (Motau, 2018).

When academic promotion criteria set in institutional policies is trampled upon in favour of scholarly mediocrity, well-deserving academics lose motivation for hard work and excellence in their trade. Under such conditions, those without the energy to fight for justice opt to invest much of their time to non-academic activities and/or simply resign from the institutions where the rot is too deep or just quit academic career. On the other hand, some under-qualified academics who are lucky to have sympathisers at the Executive Management level who also seat in internal board of assessors to consider promotion applications get it very easy. In fact, such mediocre academics are even canvased by such Executives to submit their applications for professorial promotion even though they do not meet statutory requirements. Such a coterie of academics cannot profess knowledge and instead, have mastered the art of professing ignorance and blind loyalty to those in influential offices. When one is in the good books of decision makers, even accepted manuscripts that are not yet published but are at the production stage are considered.

Ironically, the young academic X's intention to re-file an application for full professorship was shot down by his line manager on the 3rd August 2020. The decline by the line manager to consider this application was based on the fact that young academic X's PhD supervision criteria was met, but the candidate was yet to graduate. This reasons are based on technical grounds and it is neither in line with an earlier reason cited by line manager for the refusal to process the application. That this criterion is not even a statutory requirement simply reflects the extent that those who are occupying positions of power and privilege can abuse their authority to achieve short and narrow goals which add no value to the academic project. Young academic X's supervised PhD thesis was passed by external assessors as early March 2020 but the candidate could not graduate because of unexplainable reasons. In fact, Covid19 related events in the country presented some of those in positions of responsibility with an excuse to deflect accountability and sabotage junior subordinates. It is unfortunate that students get sacrificed in the process. Such acts of sabotage are seemingly geared at nothing except to hurt the supervisor (Ramaphosa, 2020). The foregoing should be understood within the context that if the student in question graduates, the reasons for denying young academic X with a professorial promotion would naturally be rendered null and void. In order to avoid having to award full professorship to a youth or someone who appear in their eyes as 'a novice academic', it may not be too far-fetched to resort to the victimisation of those that are under his supervision. Only time will tell as to how long these dirty tricks will be sustained. The reality is that the student's graduation can only be delayed but it cannot be stopped. The only short term achievement attributable to his delayed graduation is the demoralisation of the supervisor so that his aspirations to breed and/or train the next generation of scientific knowledge producers can be corroded.

Contextually, the inconsistency in handling applications for academic promotions are emblematic of the extent to which un-checked institutional autonomy can be exploited over the platter of gossip, squabbles, nepotism, corruption and related social ills that all consummate or result into a gradual and/or partial collapse of governance (Shai, 2020b). In toxic academic spaces in the higher education sector, it is not uncommon to subtly hear that "if you want to be promoted, do not talk too much". In this context "not talking too much" entails being non-critical of those who are in leadership. The latter is a serious problem as it compromises democracy of thought (also read as academic freedom) and sacrifices it to the alter of toxic patronage. What causes the spiralling of this unethical practice at a higher level can best be accounted by Edmund Burke's (as cited by Campbell, 2017) conviction: "The only thing necessary for the triumph of evil is for *good men* to *do nothing*".

Inter-varsity experiences

The concerns around the dissipating African professoriate in South Africa's higher education landscape have been over discussed and it has become a common knowledge (Higher Education Transformation

Network, 2020). While this is national problem, it is worse in HBUs. For a number of reasons (including heavy workloads, teaching responsibilities and family expectations), most African academics have difficulty in growing within the academy. This situation in turn has a negative impact on scholarly productivity. While there are national and institutional efforts to turn the situation around, such is not enough. This calls for the urgent need to sponsor Masters and PhD students *enmasse* to top universities abroad. Unfortunately, the few African academics who took this route were at the mercy of overseas universities, corporates and governments in terms of sponsorship. The sad thing is that such overseas sponsors often dictate a particular research agenda for the beneficiary as a precondition for their funding. Such a research agenda is not always in the best interests of African nations. Post-sponsorship term, it is less likely that the beneficiaries would want to grow themselves within such less relevant niche research areas. This often results in a situation wherein a PhD graduate cannot even harvest one or two journal articles from his/her thesis. Products of such circumstances do not make a meaningful contribution to enhance scientific knowledge in Africa. Consequently, they find themselves being overwhelmed by anxiety to a point wherein they naturally relegate themselves to mere university teachers who contribute nothing in terms of knowledge generation.

In the midst of untransformed spaces in the higher education sector in South Africa, there is a desperate need to commit white academics to deliberately transfer skills to Black South African academics as they exit the system. This is not happening as it should. To add, legislation should be biased and enforceable in ways that commit foreign academics to deliberately transfer skills to Black South African academics as they exit the system. This too is not happening as it should. Contextually, academic staff mobility is crucial for building and maintaining lasting partnerships at the national and international level. Such partnerships are essential for knowledge exchanges and co-authorship. But the unevenness in terms of the requirements for professorship by each university in South Africa hampers progress in this regard. Relatedly, I am reminded of academic Y who previously served as an Associate Professor at some universities in Limpopo. But when he later joined another university outside Limpopo, he could only be employed as a

Senior Lecturer. The reason was that in terms of publications, the requirements for Associate Professorship at the universities in Limpopo were low as compared to his new university (employer) at the time. The latter institution does not have a monopoly over this practice of technically demoting academics from their previous ranks. Related to this, I am reminded of academic Z who also served as an Associate Professor at the university in Limpopo but could only be appointed as a Senior Lecturer at another university in Gauteng. The reason was that in terms of organogram, the available advertised post was that of a Senior Lecturer. This rigidness in the application of recruitment rules is good. But it also has a potential to rob its enforcers of the scarce opportunity to attract seasoned scholars especially in disciplines wherein Black South Africans are under-represented (Shai, 2020b). A university in Limpopo is flexible during external recruitment. But rigid in processes pertaining to the promotion of its internal academic staff. In the recent past, an Associate Professor at the university outside Limpopo was recruited for Full Professorship at the university in Limpopo. He did not have a Masters and/or PhD completed supervision whatsoever, which is not a statutory requirement in any way. What bothers me is that the same un-statutory requirement for Professorship is used to dis-approve applications for professorial promotions by internal academic staff. But then, this is a clear case of George Orwell's *Animal Farm* where 'all animals are equal but some are more equal than others'. The cauldron of the foregoing analysis shows that unevenness in the higher education sector has a fair share to play for retarded state of scientific knowledge in South Africa (Higher Education Transformation Network, 2020).

Academic managerial class-administrative interface

University management is the embodiment and a mirror of each and every institution. In particular, university academic leaders who operate at the executive level need to lead by example in the promotion of the academic project (Mtshali, 2020). Leading by example on and off-campus will put any executive leader in a *locus standi* to encourage his/her subordinates to excel in teaching, research and community service. However, the reason why some institutions or academic units within them are not performing maximally is because the leaders are not shining stars in the faculties where they are expected to provide strategic leadership. This observation reminds me of a case at one university in South Africa wherein a male candidate without a PhD in the relevant faculty was among those recommended for possible appointment as an Executive Dean. Fortunately, this recommendation was never actioned as it had many flaws which had the potential of bringing the university project into disrepute. Besides the lack of a PhD, the candidate in question did not have a single accredited publication and/or even evidence of conference paper presentation. That he was shortlisted, interviewed and front running a female candidate who is an internationally renowned scholar is painstaking. In this situation it is also unfathomable how a competent female candidate can be front run by an unqualified male candidate in an era of women empowerment and affirmative action (Sithole & Shai, 2017). In terms of the organogram of the university, the Faculty Research Professor reports to the Executive Dean, who is supposed to provide executive strategic leadership in terms of teaching, research and community service. The anomaly of possibly appointing an academic novice who is only very old in terms of age as an Executive Dean presents immediate challenges for maintaining sound professional relations with his subordinates. Since such possible recommendations are not good for the academic project, they can only serve to relegate universities to the status of being 'glorified high schools'.

Despite the sad conditions intimated above which have the potential to undo the little gains that have been made in terms of advancing academic excellence in the sector, all hope is not lost. The University of Kwazulu Natal (UKZN) and lately, University of Pretoria (UP) have rewarded excellence by swelling their ranks of Deanery with selected youth. One can only hope that HBUs will follow suit as some are known for their entrenched discrimination on the basis of age and ethnic belonging. It cannot be correct that in some spaces academic excellence is reduced to ageism. Thus the logic behind hiring (or intention to do so) under-qualified old executives at the expense of the more active, productive and qualified ones is unimaginable. It may be safe to aver that such a tendency is more about the promotion of personal interests and less about the demands of institutional administration. I argue that any employer who has real interests in their hearts about continuity and stability of universities would realise that it is self-defeating to hire, or even show an intention to do so (substantively or on an acting basis), someone who is very extremely close to reaching the retirement age. This is even worse when such a near retiree is under-qualified and can barely match his peers at other universities. The under-qualified near retirees often suffer from inferiority complex, a phenomenon that causes them to be easily enticed by the sociology of hatred and revenge. Possibly finding themselves in situations of having to define the future of their subordinates and the future that they won't be part of. The point is; the under-qualified academic managerial class tends to pursue vindictive tendencies (Ndlovu-Gatsheni, 2017). Such tendencies only serve to frustrate the scholarly growth and development of subordinates who are not in their faction and at worst, to banish them in favour of less competent blind loyalists. Less competent blind loyalists may include school directors, heads of departments and senior lecturers who hold a PhD but cannot operationalise publishable research. While this coterie of academics cannot even harvest a simple journal article from their over ten years or so thesis, it is not uncommon to find them supervising countless doctoral candidates. This practice leaves one to wonder if indeed they have a potential to supervise and produce credible researchers at the doctoral level while they are not intellectually active. It may not be an exaggeration to submit that such questionable supervision arrangements are tantamount to what Ndlovu-Gatsheni (as cited by Brouwers and Le Ber 2020) terms *"episticide"*. Supervisors who avail themselves to this questionable practice should quickly adapt to intellectualism or submit for intellectual euthanasia by simply opting for non-academic appointments. These are the fundamental issues that directly or indirectly contribute to the dearth of scientific knowledge in Africa and if anything good is to happen, they should be confronted without any fear or favour.

Conclusion

The point of departure for this desktop chapter is Sebola's previously published article on the politics of scientific knowledge in Africa. As the chapter reaffirms the need to revisit this subject with an alternative theoretical and contextual, it identifies and explores the complex relationship between three key factors that contribute to the dearth of scientific knowledge in South Africa (case study) and Africa to a greater extent. Among others, the factors delved in include tricks for academic stagnation, inter-varsity experiences and the academic managerial class-administrative interface. Such factors have been overlooked by Sebola and his interlocutor because of a commitment to a particular narrative and space constraints, respectively. It is reiterated that the identified factors contributing to the dearth of scientific knowledge can best be understood when located within a historical and broader African context. Based on the findings of the research for this chapter, recommendations for confronting external human impediments to scholarly productivity have been discussed. In the same breath, suggestions for seizing opportunities required to improve the state of scientific knowledge in Africa have been advanced. In the final analysis, this chapter is poised to serve as a stepping stone for future research on the politics of scholarship in Africa.

References

Asante, M.K. 1990. *Kemet, Afrocentricity and Knowledge.* Trenton: Africa World Press.

Asante, M.K. 2003. Afrocentricity: *The Theory of Social Change.* Chicago: African American Images.

Asante, M.K. 2020. I Am Afrocentric and Pan-African: A Response to Tawanda Sydesky Nyawasha on Scholarship in South Africa. *Journal of Black Studies.* https://doi.org/10.1177/0021934720901602

Brouwers, A. & Le Ber, E. 2020. The Neo-Colonial Europeanization of Africa - A post-developmental perspective on the communication of the AU-EU Partnership, MSc dissertation in Sustainable Management, Uppsala University, Campus Gotland, https://www.diva-portal.org/smash/get/diva2:1445742/FULLTEXT01.pdf, accessed 5 August 2020.

Campbell, J. 2017. When good people do nothing – proverbs 24:11-12; mark 10:46-49. Https://goexplorethebible.com/blog/adults/when-good-people-do-nothing-proverbs-2411-12-mark-1046-49/, accessed, January 9.

CCMA. 2020. About Us. https://www.ccma.org.za/About-Us, accessed 05 August 2020.

Chazan, N. 1988. *Politics and Society in Contemporary Africa*. Basingstoke: Macmillan.

Higher Education Transformation Network. 2020. PRESS RELEASE: HETN WELCOMES MINISTERIAL TASK TEAM REPORT BY MOSOMA ET AL ON RECRUITMENT, RETENTION & PROGRESSION OF BLACK SA ACADEMIA, July 23.

Legodi, L.T. 2019. An exploration of China's foreign policy towards Sudan from 2006 to 2016: An Afrocentric Perspective. Unpublished Master of Arts (International Politics) dissertation, University of Limpopo.

Maleka M.S. & Shai K.B. 2016. South Africa's Post-Apartheid Foreign Policy Towards Swaziland. *Journal of Public Administration*, 51 (2): 194-204.

Maserumule, M.H. 2011. Good Governance in the New Partnership for Africa's Development (NEPAD: A Public Administration Perspective. Unpublished PhD Thesis. Pretoria: University of South Africa.

Mekoa, I. 2016. *Silent No More: Challenges Facing Black African Academics at South African Universities*. Cape Town: The Incwadi Press.

Mekoa, I. 2018. *The Battle for the Soul of South African Universities: Institutional Cultures, Racism and Ideologies*. Cape Town: Incwadi Press.

Modupe, D.S. 2003. The Afrocentric Philosophical Perspective: Narrative Outline. In Mazama, A. (Ed) *The Afrocentric Paradigm*. Trenton: Africa World Press.

Motau, T. 2018. VBS Mutual Bank investigators report to the Prudential Authority. Pretoria: South African Reserve Bank.

Mtshali, N. 2020. Three South African vice-chancellors paint a post-COVID picture for universities. https://theconversation.com/three-south-african-vice-chancellors-paint-a-post-covid-picture-for-universities-143490, August 2.

Lee, I. 2014. Publish or perish: The myth and reality of academic publishing. Language Teaching, 47(2), 250-261. doi:10.1017/S0261444811000504

Ndlovu-Gatsheni, S.J. 2017. The Emergence and Trajectories of Struggles for an 'African University': The Case of Unfinished Business of African Epistemic Decolonisation. *Kronos*, Vol 43 (1): 51-77.

Nnadozie, U.O. 2015. Coloniality and Governance in Africa in the Twenty-First Century: The Challenges of Public Administration. *Journal of Public Administration*, Vol 50 (2): 191-199.

Platt, J. 2007. Case Study. In Outhwaite, W. & Turner, S.P. (Eds). *The SAGE Handbook of Social Science Methodology*. Los Angeles: Sage Publications.

Ramaphosa, C. 2020. President Cyril Ramaphosa: Update on Coronavirus COVID-19 lockdown. https://www.gov.za/speeches/president-cyril-ramaphosa-update-coronavirus-covid-19-lockdown-30-mar-2020-0000, accessed 30 March 2020.

Sebola, M.P. 2018. Peer review, scholarship and editors of scientific publications: the death of scientific knowledge in Africa. *KOERS-Bulletin for Christian Scholarship*, Vol 83 (1):1-13.

Shai, K.B. & Mothibi, K.A. 2015. Describing pre-2009 Xenophobic Violence in South Africa: A Human right Perspective. In Sebola, M.P., Tsheola, J.P. & Mafunisa, M.J. (Eds). African Governance: Society, Human Migration, State, Xenophobia and Business Contestations. *Conference Proceedings*. 4rd SAAPAM Limpopo Chapter Annual Conference, 28-30 October 2015.

Shai K.B. 2016. An Afrocentric Critique of the United States of America's foreign policy towards Africa: The case studies of Ghana and Tanzania, 1990-2014. Unpublished PhD Thesis. Sovenga: University of Limpopo.

Shai, K.B. & Nyawasha, T.S. 2016. A critical appraisal of the post-Cold War United States of America's foreign policy towards Kenya: An Afrocentric perspective. *Commonwealth Youth and Development*, 14 (2): 151-169.

Shai, K.B. 2017. South African state capture: A symbiotic affair between business and state going bad(?), *Insight on Africa*, Vol 9(1): 1–14.

Shai, K.B; Nyawasha, T.S. & Ndaguba, E.A. 2018. [De] constructing South Africa's Jacob Zuma led ANC: An Afrocentric perspective. *Journal of Public Affairs*. https://doi.org/10.1002/pa.1842

Shai, K.B. 2019a. The death of scientific knowledge in [South] Africa: An Afrocentric response to M.P. Sebola. *Journal of Public Affairs.* e1975. https://doi.org/10.1002/pa.1975

Shai, K.B. 2019b. [Un]masking Sebola's Mythology on the Politics of Scholarship in South Africa: An Afrocentric Youth Perspective. *Journal of Gender, Information and Development in Africa,* Vol 8 (3): 169-185.

Shai, K.B. 2020a. Mokoko Sebola on 'Scientific Knowledge in Africa': An Afrocentric Critique. *African Renaissance,* Vol 17 (1): 143-156.

Shai, K.B. 2020b. An Afrocentric Exploration of the nexus between Sebola's *politricks* of scholarship and [South] Africa's politics of the Doctoral Project. *Journal of African Union Studies,* Vol 9 (2): 89-106.

Sithole, T.N. & Shai, K.B. 2017. Un-blurring the myths and realities of women and children's rights in South Africa. *Commonwealth Youth and Development.* Vol 14 (2): 109-120.

CHAPTER SIX

Politicisation of university administration and implications for knowledge development in South Africa

Introduction

The subject of the dichotomy between politics and administration is not new within the scholarly circles. In particular, it has been a hotbed of academic debate among the scholars emanating from Public Administration, Political Science, and their sister disciplines. Despite its old age, the debate about the politicisation or de-politicisation of administration remains deeply polarised (Author, 2019c). This is especially the case when the debate relates to the government and/or administration of public service or state. Given that universities are deemed to be an epitome of professionalism in society, one would hope that meritocracy trumps politics in their operations. But the extent literature and the practical realities on the ground tell the opposite (Maake, 2011b; Mekoa, 2016). Just like in any group interaction, politics plays an upper hand in terms of academic recruitment, retention, and promotion; appointments at the administration, oversight, and ceremonial level, funding and facilities for the academic project, honorary awards and tenders (Mushemeza, 2016; Netswera, 2016). In this context, politics is loosely conceptualised and contextualised as the power struggle that may manifest at the personal, ethnic, race, partisan, and/or any other form. The influence of politics in this regard is real but it is often downplayed or ignored because the universities are largely autonomous (Sebola, 2019). Institutional autonomy within the higher education sector is not at all bad. What is bad is the tendency in certain universities to use institutional autonomy as a cover-up for wrongdoing in management circles. In the case of South Africa, it is extremely unjustifiable especially if one is to consider the fact that most universities are public owned and they are highly subsidised with public funds. Therefore, unchecked institutional autonomy is problematic.

I am aware of the existence of councils as the oversight bodies of governance at the South African universities. Unfortunately, some of these councils are constituted in a manner that is vulnerable to manipulation. The latter often produces councils that are not truly independent of management. Often, terms of Vice-Chancellors are extended beyond a decade without a sound basis. This is because there is nothing progressive and/or substantive that a person (in executive management) can still offer that he or she could not offer in ten years. As such, there is no justification for such extension and because they know, they do not even bother to furnish reasons for such to the members of the university community or the country as a whole. It is such manipulative tendencies that have led some universities to become personal fiefdoms of Vice-Chancellors and such abnormality thrives through unchecked institutional autonomy. It is unchecked because council members include old political rejects and careless members of the Students Representative Council (SRC) who are easily manipulated through financial resources. On one hand, government or ministerial representatives hardly makes it to council meetings where critical decisions are made. Those who represent Senate in the council are members of management in their own right and to a certain extent, beholden to the Vice Chancellors. At times and in total disregard of institutional statues, senate representatives in council are self-appointed and presented to senate for ratification. These mischivious practices are hardly challenged in senate meetings due to prevailing conditions of fear for reprissals by those command the chain of power at the universities. On the other hand, those who represent convocation, business, or just the community have proven to want to toe the line in return for benefiting from the evil patronage system that is presided by the Vice-Chancellors and their lieutenants (Netswera, 2016).

The foregoing discourse has been researched in other parts of the world including Africa (Edet, Asuguo & Okon, 2020). A few studies in the case of South Africa has been conducted (Mashabela, 2011; Mekoa, 2018). However, the existing body of knowledge on these issues has not adequately taken account of the case of a contemporary Black university in South Africa. Hence, there is a misguided view that Black universities are transformed since their leadership, workforce and student population are predominantly Black (Pittaway, 2019). They tend to get sympathy from the government, private sector, civil society, and members of the public to a point of not giving much attention to their unethical practices that are prevalent within their ranks (Netswera, 2016; Nzimande, 2020). Against this background, this conceptual chapter uses a rural Black university in South Africa as a test case to reflect on key challenges that emanate from the politicisation of university administration and the extent to which they affect the generation and development of scientific knowledge in Africa. This chapter is an extension of my previous works on this subject (Author, 2019a; Author, 2019b; Author, 2020a; Author, 2020b). Due to space constraints, I could not exhaust the list of these challenges. Even now, it is not possible to do so. But this chapter is poised to enrich the existing body of knowledge on this subject. Of particular importance to note is that this chapter is written from a victim's point of view. This is achieved by employing Afrocentricity as a contextual and theoretical lens (Asante, 2003; Legodi&Shai, 2020). Besides its cognitive abilities, Afrocentricity has the functional attributes that puts it at the edge in terms of identifying and addressing any forms of inequities and injustices that have a bearing on the livelihood of the Africans including those whose fate is tied to the rural Black university under scrutiny (Mazama, 2003).

It is worth noting that the challenges delved in this chapter have less to do with the university's (study focus) Black orientation and geographic location. There is absolutely nothing wrong about the university that broadly services Blacks, who are in any way the majoritarian segment of the South African population. Equally, there is nothing untoward about the university being situated in a rural location. In fact, the location of such institutions in rural areas should be encouraged as they provide opportunities for socio-economic development. This should be understood within the context that the fast growth of towns such as Thohoyandou and Polokwane cannot be delinked from their status as the host towns of the two main universities in Limpopo. Contextually, what is a problem is when the identity of being a rural Black university is exploited to swing the politics of administration in a direction that retards the institution's potential to make a meaningful contribution towards scientific knowledge (Netswera, 2016).

Research findings and discussion[5]

Bureaucratisation of academic administration

There is no gainsaying that the breeding of postgraduate students (especially at Masters and Doctoral level) is a rich investment for the future with enhanced scientific knowledge. Unfortunately, a Black university in South Africa is not performing as it should in terms of the production of quality graduates at the post-graduate level. The number of post-graduates admitted into different post-graduate qualifications is far higher than those that successfully exit them (Council on Higher Education, 2019). Some students drop out of their studies before they could even go beyond the proposal stage. Those who are lucky to survive the proposal approval processes and stay in the system, often do not complete their studies in record time. One of the reasons that are less talked about for the delayed completion of post-graduate qualifications at the Black university is the redundancy of research and ethics committees. Before a student would be allowed to operationalise his/her study s/he is expected to successfully present and defend the proposal at the various research and ethics committees at the departmental, school, faculty, and central level. Even as and when the study is completed, the assessment reports need to go through such a convoluted committee system for approval before the student can graduate. The argument that is often advanced to justify such a convoluted committee system is that of quality assurance and enhancement (Author, 2020b). But those who are fortunate to serve in these committees will attest that much of their work amounts to duplication of efforts. While disciplinary expertise in terms of proposal

---

[5] This chapter is not necessarily a representation of my personal [his]story as an academic. But it is more of a scholarly recollection and reflection of the silenced voices. Therefore, this chapter should be broadly seen as an expression of the silenced and marginalised voices in the higher education sector in South Africa. Some of the silenced voices have confided to me and it is on this basis that they are referred in the chapter as character/ academic A, B and etc.

adjudication rests with departments, the truth of the matter is that the further the proposal is adjudicated far from its home department, the less likely it is to get relevant inputs or let alone, a fair evaluation. This observation should not be mistaken to disregard the value of interdisciplinarity in research. But even in cases where interdisciplinarity is the way, such can never supersede disciplinary bases (Author, 2020a). While this sentiment and the extent to which the longevity of the proposal approval process at the university is recognised, power politics reigns supreme in discussions that seek to de-establish research and ethics committees at certain levels. For example, those who lead faculty research and ethics committees are often reluctant to devolve much power to departments. It is ironic that before some proposals are given final approval and ethical clearance, they would have been seen many similar academics for about three times but in different capacities and at different levels.

While the argument for quality assurance and enhancement in these processes is sensible; they also need to be interrogated with a historical lens (Asante, 1990). This is because the proposal approval processes at elite universities (which are largely white) are generally short. This does not imply poor quality of proposals processed at these universities. But it is reflective of an appreciation that a proposal is nothing but a rough blueprint of a proposed study. The undeclared logic of the longevity of the proposal approval process at a Black university was previously conceived for the sole purpose of demoralising and frustrating Black students so that they lose the urge to further their studies at the post-graduate level. The fact that such un-progressive systems are now defended and promoted by Black academic leaders leaves one with a question of whose interests do they serve. Obviously, it cannot be interests of the Black community whose children are prejudiced by this very same system.

Amid the crisis of the ageing professoriate in South Africa, it is not uncommon to hear university academics invoking the line of "growing our own timber" (Higher Education Transformation Network, 2020). This line implies the identification of doctoral students within the university community, enrolling them internally, and mentoring them to assume future academic appointments/ promotions at the same university. While this might have good intentions, it is also having a downside. In fact, its excessive application can lead to inbreeding, which is not so good for the much-needed internationalisation of higher education. On the other hand, the principle of "growing our own timber" is at times failed by those who are entrusted with the responsibility to advocate it. This contradiction can be referred to as the 'hidden hand of the academic managerial class' or administration over-reach. In this regard, I am reminded of a situation in one Black university in South Africa wherein a school higher degrees' committee approved a student's[6] doctoral proposal in a session that was not honoured by the substantive committee chairperson, who was also the head of the school. For reasons that are beyond the comprehension of this chapter, the school director opted to read the proposal in question outside the formal processes and came to a conclusion that was in contrast to the pronouncement by the properly committed school higher degrees' committee. The sad part was that such a school director neither had a Ph.D. or impressive research publications record (Maake, 2011b). But she was allowed to review doctoral proposals in a school that she presided over. Clearly, the two conflicting verdicts on the doctoral proposal derailed the affected student's progress. Considering that the student in question needed the signature of the school head/ director for his proposal to move to the next level, he opted not to appeal. But he simply revised the proposal to address the concerns of the school director, even though such concerns did not have a scholarly/ disciplinary basis. When the proposal was cleared, the student then threw away the proposal with a double consciousness and operationalised the study as per originally shared understanding with his supervisors and the school's higher degrees committee. The academic mediocrity as demonstrated above can best be captured by what NhlanhlaMaake (2011a) terms *Barbarism in Higher Education*.

It is worth highlighting that in a Black university under scrutiny there are no clear guidelines for appeal procedure in the treatment of research proposals. Managerial cronyism and unhealthy respect for authority at the expense of scholarly prowess is what a student mostly needs to progress academically. In such instances, higher degrees' committee meetings are times degenerating into "Kangaroo courts". In this regard, I

---

[6] Such a student was also a lecturer at the same university.

am reminded of an appeal about the review of a proposal by the higher degrees committee which was violently quashed without the decency to advance scholarly justification. Among the baseless reasons used to disapprove such a student's proposal was its adoption of Afrocentricity as a theory when the committee deemed Afrocentricity to be just an attitude. This polemic is outdated and those internationally renowned scholars who stand for Afrocentricity have won the day (Asante, 2020). So it comes as a surprise that the higher degrees committee at a Black university that ought to promote the African thought system will make pronouncements that conflict with what they ought to stand for. This calls for another wave of self-introspection by Black universities. Such exercise should go beyond apportioning empty accolades towards one another. The point of truly identifying your scholarly weaknesses is to give yourself the best chance to transcend them. Unlike in a Black university where the difference in opinions attracts denial of study completion for the student or promotion on the part of the supervisor, some universities are normalising the practice of robust debate and academic freedom. For example, Professor Jane Duncan of the University of Johannesburg wrote a newspaper article criticising her Vice-Chancellor and Principal, Prof TshilidziMarwala. That is normal and acceptable at the University of Johannesburg and she won't be disciplined or victimised for it. This is such an environment that partly contributes to the good performance of the University of Johannesburg in terms of research outputs as compared to most Black universities in South Africa (Department of Higher Education and Training, 2020). Returning to the poor adjudication of research proposals in certain committees, I add that the paucity of discipline experts who are well-grounded in research rob this forum of enriched intellectual debate. What happens at times is that inasmuch as committees may err, the concerned lecturers/supervisors do not make things either easy as they sometimes display arrogance without clear and solid facts. This becomes even worse when both supervisor and co-supervisor are old in terms of age, but they unconsciously remain novice scholars (also read as emerging researchers).

Academic jealousy and *gangsterism*

Academic jealousy and gangsterism has both a qualitative and quantitative effect on the production of scientific knowledge and general stability of our universities (Maake, 2011a). In a Black university for example, junior academics in one multi-disciplinary department would gang up, table and adopt motions that make it difficult to forge inter-disciplinary collaboration in terms of post-graduate students research supervisions and publications. Related to this, I am reminded of an academic mob in one department at the Black university which resolved that a History Professor cannot engage in the supervision of Politics postgraduate students. Ironically, this is a Professor who had a wealth of postgraduate supervision experience and at the time of this moratorium, he had already successfully supervised no less 5 PhD graduates who were really doing well in their trades. If one is to closely look at this populist resolution, it is clearly not in the best interest of scientific knowledge. Hence, the 'careless' disqualification of the History Professor in the supervision of Politics students had left many students without a supervisor.[7] Even those who had one in the area of Politics, he was inexperienced in terms of doctoral research supervision and also over-burdened with unbearable teaching and post-graduate supervision load. At the end, it is post graduate supervision progress that suffered which in turn negatively affects the state of scientific knowledge in South Africa. In certain instances, such gansterism escalate to a point wherein senior academics are even overlooked during the voting for Departmental Headship in favour of inexperienced junior colleagues.

This form of gangsterism is not limited to one campus of Black university. It could be observed in other Black campuses in South Africa. I am reminded of one over rated and old Philosophy Professor who supervised a Masters student in History, a discipline that is foreign to him. He went out to publish a memoir wherein he was criticising the

---

[7] I refer to this moratorium as careless because it fails to recognise that the provincialisation of academic disciplines is a Western construct. In an African thought system and real sense, there is a closer relationship between History and Political Science. Thus, History is broadly understood as the study of the politics of the past. On the other hand, Political Science may denote the study of the history of the present (Hirst, 1985).

supervision of a Masters student in Philosophy by a junior Philosopher and a Senior Political Scientist (More, 2019). This type of hypocrisy is reflective of the extent to which some academics are hell-bent on advancing cheap, narrow and selfish arguments to make a living irrespective of the potential damage of their conspiracies to the knowledge industry. This is even concerning when a senior academic goes out to rent a national mob of sympathetic cheerleaders to lend credence to his so called "un-pleasurable experience" at the Black university. What can be deduced from the foregoing is that the demon of ambition, ambition to rule and refusal to be ruled even when your days are numbered, is what kills some senior academics' prospects of transferring their skills to the next generation of scientific knowledge producers. In the same Black university, there is a sense by some seasoned scholars that there is concerted effort right from the Office of the School Director to Head of Department to overload their opponents with teaching and learning work. Apparently, this could be explained by the fact that the school and departmental management seems not to value research, particularly the one that is being carried by academic A.[8] Even at the so called research intensive universities, it is not uncommon to hear laments for the over-burdening of academics with teaching and learning responsibilities. Such conditions are obviously not good for the sustained production of scientific knowledge by those who are at the receiving end of such unbearable working conditions.

Sadly, the conception of some academic line managers is that real academic work is only confined to teaching and learning only. To them, research (independent) and postgraduate supervision is not real work but luxury. The mixture of such a shallow thinking and/or poor grasp of scholarly issues is typical of the academic managerial class; which mostly served in the past as basic school teachers/ principals and they have difficulty of shedding away their elementary school tendencies.[9] What can be deduced from the foregoing is that personnel with no clue whatsoever

---

[8] The true identity is withheld for ethical reasons.

[9] Such draconian tendencies include the policing of academics in a manner that basic Bantustan school principals and inspectors monitored their subordinates especially during the heydays of apartheid in South Africa. When such practices are transplanted in the higher education sector, Black universities are running a risk of being relegated to the status of glorified high schools.

about research are accidently finding themselves making key decisions that directly affects researchers and their trade, at times in a bad way. Related to this, I recall of an instance wherein a Faculty Dean of one Black university disapproved an academic participation in a fully externally funded conference attendance. The reason for such a disapproval was that the conference was happening during the exam time. That arrangements were already made for someone to be responsible for academic B's work for the 2 days of the conference could not be entertained by those who have executive authority; which they clearly abuse to deny their subordinates to make a meaningful contribution to scholarly discourse in South Africa. Besides the fact that research is a valuable independent variable, what emerges from the above is also emblematic of its positive influence in quality teaching and status in terms of community engagement/ service. Indeed, the failure to integrate the Black university's core functions of teaching and learning, research and community engagement in the understanding of the academic managerial class is regrettable and warrants a serious intervention by those entrusted with quality assurance and enhancement competencies.

Shortage of academic role models

In a Black university there is a shortage of post-graduate supervisors who fit the label of 'role models (Higher Education Transformation Network, 2020). Some of the academics who are involved in postgraduate supervision do not possess terminal qualifications; which means they are limited in terms of their abilities to inspire students under their supervision to study until the doctoral level. Beyond the writing of their Masters dissertations, such students are not inspired to produce other research outputs such as conference papers, journal articles, book chapters, monographs and etc (Department of Higher Education and Training, 2020). Hence, most of their supervisors are research inactive to inspire scholarly confidence and publication. Students who find themselves under supervision of research inactive academics are often subjected to baseless reminders for them to just focus on their dissertations until they complete their studies. By the time students complete their studies, they are dissertation fatiqued and have no interest to publish. But they need jobs to make a living. To compound matters to an already worse situation, serious scholars find themselves at the mercy of Faculty Executive Teams (FETs) before they could be favoured with a promotion reward system for academic excellence. Unfortunately, FETs are not always meant for scholars of good standing. Some of the them do not even have as little two sound research outputs that are accredited by the Department of Higher Education and Training in South Africa. Yet, such members of FETs (also referred to as the academic managerial class) should provide higher strategic leadership in terms of research excellence.

Conclusion

Based on qualitative materials and discourse analysis, this chapter has identified three key challenges that emanate from the politicisation of university administration and discussed the extent to which they affect the generation and development of scientific knowledge in South Africa. The point of departure for the thesis of this chapter was existing body of knowledge (including the previous works of the current author) on this subject. This chapter has enriched its discourse by blending an insider's perspective with the recollection of the experiences of the past and present victims of unethical academic conduct, which has corroded the knowledge industry in South Africa and Africa as a whole. Emerging from this discourse, it is clear that the findings of this chapter will inform the thinking within university corridors and government circles in terms of the best ways to create an enabling environment for sustainable research record and academic excellence. Lastly, this chapter is poised to serve as a stepping stone for future research on this subject. The study could be replicated by focusing on other Black universities in South Africa or elsewhere.

References

Asante, M.K. 1990. *Kemet, Afrocentricity and Knowledge*. Trenton: Africa World Press.

Asante MK. 2003. Afrocentricity: *The Theory of Social Change*. Chicago: African American Images.

Asante MK. 2020. I Am Afrocentric and Pan-African: A Response to TawandaSydeskyNyawasha on Scholarship in South Africa. *Journal of Black Studies*.

Author. 2019a. The death of scientific knowledge in [South] Africa: An Afrocentric response to M.P. Sebola. *Journal of Public Affairs*. e1975. https://doi.org/10.1002/pa.1975

Author. 2019b. [Un]maskingSebola's Mythology on the Politics of Scholarship in South Africa: An Afrocentric Youth Perspective. *Journal of Gender, Information and Development in Africa*, Vol 8 (3): 169-185.

Author. 2019c. The Paradox of (De)politicisation in a Selected South African Municipality: An Afrocentric Ethical Reflection. *Politeia* 38 (2), 12 pages. https://doi.org/10.25159/2663-6689/6088.

Author. 2020a. MokokoSebola on 'Scientific Knowledge in Africa': An Afrocentric Critique. *African Renaissance*, Vol 17 (1): 143-156.

Author.2020b. An Afrocentric exploration of the nexus between Sebola's*politricks* of scholarship and [South] Africa's politics of the Doctoral Project.*Journal of African Union Studies*, Vol 9 (2): 89-106.

Council on Higher Education. 2019. VitalStats, Public Higher Education, 2017. Pretoria: Council on Higher Education.

Department of Higher Education and Training. 2020. Report on the Evaluation of 2018 Universities' Research Output. Pretoria: Department of Higher Education and Training.

Edet AO; Asuguo ME.&Okon JE. 2020. Academic Staff Perception of the Extent of Politicizing Administration of Universities: Implications for National Development. *Mediterranean Journal of Social Sciences*, Vol 11 (4): 38-48.

Higher Education Transformation Network. 2020. Press Release: HETN Welcomes Ministerial Task Team Report By Mosoma Et Al On Recruitment, Retention & Progression of Black SA Academia, July 23.

Hirst PQ. 1985. *Marxism and Historical Writing.* London and New York: Routledge&Kegan Paul.

Legodi L T &Shai KB. 2020. [Re]Visiting Molefe Kete Asante's Theory of Afrocentricity. In S. Zondi (ed.). *African Voices: In Search of a Decolonial Turn.* Pretoria: Africa Institute of South Africa, pp. 151-167.

Maake, N. 2011a.*Barbarism in Higher Education: Once Upon a Time in a University.* Johannesburg: Ekaam Books.

Maake, N. 2011b.*Hyenas in a place of joy.*Johannesburg: Ekaam Books.

Mashabela NT. 2011. Is democracy possible in university governance? A case of the University of Limpopo.*South African Journal of Higher Education,* Vol 25 (8): 1581-1591.

Mazama A. (Ed). 2003. *The Afrocentric Paradigm.* Trenton: Africa World Press.

Mekoa I. 2016.*Silent No More: Challenges Facing Black African Academics at South African Universities.* Cape Town: The Incwadi Press.

Mekoa I. 2018.*The Battle for the Soul of South African Universities: Institutional Cultures, Racism and Ideologies.* Cape Town: Incwadi Press.

More MP. 2019. *Looking Through Philosophy in Black: Memoirs.* London:Rowman& Littlefield International.

Mushemeza ED. 2016. Opportunities and Challenges of Academic Staff in Higher Education in Africa.*International Journal of Higher Education,* Vo. 5 (3): 236-246.

Netswera F. 2016. Why you don't want to become 'another Turfloop'. *PoliticsWeb,* https://www.politicsweb.co.za /opinion/why-you-dont-want-to-become-another-turfloop (accessed May 11).

Nzimande BE. 2020. The Minister of Higher Education, Science and Innovation, Dr Blade Nzimande's Statement on "Covid-19 Alert Level 2 Measures in the Post School Education and Training Sector", 26 August 2020.

Pittaway, D. 2019. Know they Systemic Enemies: Mechanisms that Prevent Transformation. *Politikon,* Vol 46 (3): 326-244.

Sebola MP. 2019. Governance and Student Leadership in South African Universities: Co-governing with Those to Be Governed. *Journal of Gender, Information and Development in Africa,* Vol 8 (2): 7-18.

CHAPTER SEVEN

Tawanda Nyawasha on Changing Scholarship in South Africa: An Afrocentric critique

Introduction

Tawanda Sydesky Nyawasha's (2019) paper entitled "'I am of Popper', 'I am of Asante': The Polemics of Scholarship in South Africa" is thought provoking. It is also a welcome and substantial addition to the evolving discourse on the politics of scholarship in South Africa (Maserumule, 2015; Sebola, 2018; Shai, 2019). This article was published in a high impact factor journal: *Studies in Philosophy and Education*. The latter does not in any way suggests that Nyawasha'spaper offers a novel contribution to the subject of this paper. In fact, his paper regurgitates the already known and baseless negativities that have been unleashed against Afrocentricity (Shai, 2016). The stronghold of the anti-Afrocentric agenda is in the West, especially in the United States of America (USA) (Carruthers, 1999). What is particularly puzzling about Nyawasha's paper is that its author is an African of Zimbabwean origin.[10] Assuming that ancestors can read, former Zimbabwean President Robert Mugabe should be turning in his grave. Hence, Nyawasha's positionality on the subject of scholarship in South Africa has a potential to speak life to colonialism and imperialism of Africa's knowledge economy, the very evils that Mugabe and his contemporaries devoted their entire lives to fight and defeat (Hussein, 1998). This is because the usual nemesis of the Afrocentric discourse are Euro-Americans. While my response to Nyawasha's paper is not necessarily an attack on his persona, it important for me to highlight a few points about him which should assist the reader to gain a greater sense of what informs his views about

---

[10]This identification is not meant to set one nationality against the other. But it is an undisputed fact that the reader ought to know in order to understand the positionality of Nyawasha and the broader context of his writing.

Afrocentricity and the context of my response. Nyawasha is a Senior Lecturer in Sociology at the university in Limpopo, where I am currently based. He is also my friend and before I penned this synthesis, I requested a permission from him and he reluctantly agreed. His reluctance was informed by the fact that he has suffered enough intellectual bruises from Asante's (2020) rejoinder and he was still grappling with the idea of writing a possible rejoinder. Only time will tell as to whether such a rejoinder will be penned and made available to the public. Inasmuch as he is my friend, I still feel that I should respond to his initial submission about the Afrocentric idea. The idea is not to intellectually incapacitate him but to engage him so that his research, writing and post-graduate supervision can be locally relevant and globally competitive. This envisaged possibility is drawn from the economic theory of comparative advantage (Landsburg, 2020). Nyawasha should know better that in the Westernised epistemology, he will forever be an emerging scholar. The chances of becoming an established scholar and match those who have been socialised at it (Westernised epistemology) from the wombs of their mothers is nil. It is only in the Afrocentric discourse wherein he stands to comparatively compete because it is the Afrocentric idea that he was first immersed to at pre-birth stages of his life.

He is currently attached to an indefensible epistemic cause whose refusal to coexist with Afrocentricity constitute an imminent threat to the democracy of thought of Nyawasha's descendants and future generations of Africans (Maserumule, 2015). My chapter seeks to identify and address the scholarly weaknesses in Nyawasha's paper. While Asante (2020) has ably done this, my qualms with his response is its sophistry. His defense of Afrocentricity is pitched at a higher level and I wish to complement it by adding a view from Limpopo. It cannot be correct that a serious issue about the state of scholarship in South Africa is discussed between Nyawasha (Zimbabwean) and Asante (USA national) while South Africans are mum. It should be categorically stated that while Nyawasha is affiliated to South Africa's university in Limpopo, as Black South Africans, we do not identify ourselves with his views as demonstrated hereunder. My response may not necessarily represent the views of all South Africans, but it is poised to give the reader a greater sense of the dominant voice in Limpopo. This is the very voice that has welcomed Nyawasha with winds of change on campus as he returned from a four-year sabbatical in China.

A born again or hypocrite: A struggle to understand Nyawasha's intellectual orientation

In his paper that I am responding to, Nyawasha hopelessly attempts to kill the Afrocentric idea. He rejects Afrocentricity and label it as a "false" theory. What emerges from this is that Nyawasha is intellectually confused. Therefore, he does not have moral *locus standi* to clear confusion around the Afrocentric discourse. Clearly, he cannot draw a distinction between Afrocentricity (theory) and Afrocentricism (ideology). Afrocentricity is not the opposite of Eurocentrism (Asante, 2003). He also fails to appreciate the nexus between theory, ideology and philosophy. While this confusion is loud in his current paper, one wonders as to what might have gone wrong with his mind. Nyawasha has previously co-published no less than two papers in the *Journal of Public Affairs* and *Commonwealth Youth and Development*, all of which we underpinned by the theory of Afrocentricity (Shai & Nyawasha, 2016; Shai, Nyawasha & Ndaguba, 2018). He also co-supervises revolutionary doctoral students whose research work is also foregrounded on Afrocentricity. A combination of this backs a question of consistency in his research and writing. It would appear that he sympathises with Afrocentricity or dismisses it when it is convenient for him. This form of inconsistency is tantamount to intellectual dishonesty. It shows a desperate desire on his part to demolish Afrocentricity, yet leave a room to receive scholarly benefits that it presents.

On a very sad note

To recap, Nyawasha introduces his paper with a quote from Ian Hacking who submits that fundamental scholarly differences among academics cause fierce conflicts among them. Such conflicts are believed to even cause colleagues not to talk to each other. This observation by Hacking (as cited by Nyawasha) is certainly based on his lived experience and in a specific context. But it is unfortunate that such an observation is now generalised. For example, myself and Nyawasha have deep-seated differences when it comes to questions of epistemology and ontology. The same could be said when both of us previously disagreed with a Senior colleague in Psychology in terms of what constitute "data". Although the debate was heated, we all laughed off at the end of our school's research and ethics committee and we continue to relate well. Hence, we are intellectually mature and have a full understanding that knowledge can only be bettered through the contestation of ideas and not the shrillness of conformity.

There is no gainsaying that Nyawasha's paper is structurally ridiculous. He draws heavily from scholars such as Karl Popper, Thomas Kuhn and Paul Feyerabend, *inter alia* to make his argument. This is a serious problem that in Nyawasha's mind the models of intellectual greatness are whites only. To show that he has erred a lot in his paper, he could not find a single African to concretely back up his argument as part of the literature consulted. Nyawasha also uses the essays of students who are still learning as a launching pad for his attack on Afrocentricity. He fails to reveal whether the students whose essays he cites were allowed to proceed with their research using the theory of Afrocentricity. He also leaves us with serious questions as to whether those students had graduated, in record time or not. Nyawasha also makes a reference to colleagues; I guess he includes me and a former colleague who is a die-hard proponent of Afrocentricity. Unfortunately, Nyawasha simply casts aspersions on our academic soundness without favouring the readership of *Studies in Philosophy and Education* with details about our works. Omissions of crucial information of this nature in Nyawasha's paper lend credence to my belief that the argument of his paper was not well thought. Even though his paper is emphatically published in a high impact factor journal, the fact that the peer reviewers of his paper and the editor of the outlet that published it overlooked such grey areas, raises so many questions than answers. It may not be too farfetched to aver that the editor and his peer reviewers may be white and the dramatization of African self-hate in Nyawasha's paper blinded thoroughness in their work. Related to this, the choice and use of words such as 'epistemological narcism' is concerning. It cannot be correct that when Africans strive to find their voice in academic writing, such is then ridiculed by scholars like Nyawasha as 'epistemological narcism'. In Afrocentricity, Africans have found a cogent idea that they can well relate with. This is the idea that they take pride in and its experimentation over time has produced a solid evidence to justify its existence and application (Chilisa, 2012). Considering that like any idea, for an Afrocentric idea to be sustainable, it requires full confidence in it by its advocates (Robbins, 2016). If this observation is to be accepted as correct, it is then safe to assert that Nyawasha's paper serves the purpose of ridiculing our epistemic confidence as self-flattery and arrogance. Such an agenda's strategic intent can only benefit those who believe in the maintenance of white supremacy, whiteness and white privilege (Shai, 2019).

In his paper, Nyawasha contradicts himself and in several instances, he stands on the intellectual fence/ middle ground. This is because his argument is extremely weak and it cannot stand on its own. For example, Nyawasha notes that in the subject of this paper, there are two camps: one that supports the continued use existing major theoretical approaches or canons; and the other that propagates for their displacement with new/ alternative theories. Elsewhere in the paper, Nyawasha introduces a third camp represented by those who stand for the complementarity of Afrocentricity and non-African theories (also read as Euro-American theories). He argues that the location of Afrocentricity in inter-disciplinarity constitutes a self-inflicted intellectual injury. Hence, such a move indirectly concedes that Afrocentricity cannot stand on its own and it offers nothing new safe to say it is a variant of social constructivism.

It is my well-considered view that like all theories, Afrocentricity is not beyond critique. In contributing to this debate through a seminal work on Afrocentricity as a theory of social change, Asante (2003: 56) notes that:

> Afrocentricity can stand its ground among any ideology or religion. Your Afrocentricity will emerge in the presence of other ideologies because it is from you. It is a truth, even though it may not be their truth.

The invocation of the above expression in this section of the chapter does not in any way suggest that Afrocentricity is an ideology. Even if it can be erroneously considered in certain circles as an ideology; herein it is employed as a theory and guiding tool to study any phenomena through an Afrocentric lens. Being Afrocentric has everything with framing the research in a manner that is pro-African interests, on the bases of African history and culture and centering it on Africa (Asante, 2003). It is also important to note that ideologies are derived on theories and in the same vein, theories are reinforced by ideologies (Shai, 2016).

To o ensure that my chapter is not only informative but also educative, I now pause to provide a conceptual clarification of the key terms that Nyawasha laments are used loosely by Afrocentricists to characterise Afrocentricity. I also extend my discussion, by expanding on the relationship of these terms. Theory is a well-developed and relatively consistent set of ideas that is based on both logic and empirical information which is observable. Philosophy is also a consistent and systematic set of ideas that is purely based on logic. On the other hand, ideology is a well-developed and relatively consistent set of ideas that have a sufficient number of adherents to have a social impact (Shai, 2015). Emerging from this, it is clear that Afrocentricity well qualifies as a theory. Closer to this, Afrocentricism will fit as an ideology while Pan-Africanism qualify for either an ideology or philosophy depending on the context of its usage. Thus, a combination of Afrocentricity, Afrocentricism, Pan-Africanism and Afrocentric research methodology constitute a wide body knowledge known as a paradigm (Afrocentric). The Afrocentric paradigm is rooted within the African world view (Mazama, 2003). Flowing from the foregoing observasion, Mkabela (2005: 184) outlines the aims of the Afrocentric paradigm as follows:

- To ensure development of an African-centred perspective
- To ensure that ethics are culturally defined; and have an indigenous African code
- To create guidelines and ensure genuine incorporation of indigenous African views in such documents
- To ensure research methods and styles are culturally acceptable.

According to Reviere (2001: 710) "the researcher is expected to examine and to place in the foreground of the enquiry any and all subjectivities or societal baggage that would otherwise remain hidden and, hence, covertly influence research activity." In his paper, Nyawasha fails in this daunting task of our time wherein we need to acknowledge the dirty history of the so called universal theories such as Marxism. Unlike

Afrocentricity, Marxism only applies in explaining the relationship between the working class and those who own the means of production (Shai, 2016). But it also has its limitations especially if one is to recognise the undisputed truth that Marxism is based on the experiences of Europe. In dismissing Afrocentricitity as a theory and its attendant cousins, Nyawasha used irrelevant and highly debated concepts such as validity. This does not apply to us and in fact it does not find a true and honest expression in the Afrocentric thought system and knowledge structure (Milam, 1992). It is displaced by credibility. The very notion of "true or false theory" is theoretical in its own right. Therefore, Nyawasha's narrow conception of what a theory and what a theory is not has been pre-empted by Asante (2003) when he cautioned that Africans should be careful not to be boxed or "trapped" (my addition) in concepts whose very origin was informed by non-African thought systems and knowledges. Related to this, Nyawasha (p. 5) correctly points out that "Afrocentricity also makes an assumption that knowledge is grounded or 'centred' in a particular place". The fact is simply thrown by Nyawasha without engaging with it. This tendency cannot be delinked from the general attitude he displays throughout the paper of failing to take a position and to justify it. Hence, he is equally confused by a simple act of working against the epistemic identity that he was born with and which he now unconsciously and un-ceremoniously shedding so that he can be relevant to those who control and manage the knowledge structure of the global political economy (Euro-American powers and people) (Shai, 2017).

From his paper, Nyawasha also emphatically confuses theory (Afrocentricity) with methodology (Afrocentric research methodology). Without going to details about his nebulous argument in this regard, he loses sight of the centrality of the researcher in the conceptualisation and operationalisation of studies. Afrocentric studies dismiss the empty perceptual space between the researcher and the researched (Milam, 1992). This is because data cannot speak, it cannot write and all these roles are performed by the researcher whose acts are all informed by particular ideological and cultural orientation (Asante, 2003). This is a reality which is not limited to qualitative or non-empirical research, it also occurs in quantitative and empirical studies, yet it is less acknowledged by those who subscribe to the Euro-American thought system. After all, Afrocentric studies rejects the binary standing of knowledge as either empirical or non-empirical, qualitative or quantitative because the complexity of contemporary societal problems requires all these traditions to reinforce one another if sustainable solutions are to be found (Maserumule, 2011). The foregoing observation should be understood within the context that the choice of a theory is a major decision that is to affect all other processes including data collection and analysis, and the place and role of the researcher in this regard. While purported inability of Afrocentricity in transferability is a major discomfort for Nyawasha, little does he know that besides transferability, dependability and confirmability is also factored in an Afrocentric discourse (Shai, 2016).

In trying to theorise quality assurance criteria in Afrocentric scholarship, Reviere (2001: 720) has invoked that "the Afrocentrist must strive for the encouragement and maintenance of harmonious relationships between groups". While Reviere's (2001: 720) invocation is an essential test for the credibility and transferability of Afrocentric studies; it is safe to state that traditional Euro-American studies are starved of such important element. Afrocentricity has ability to help us understand any phenomena in the world. It is easy for scholars such as Nyawasha to deny this because of the lack of knowledge that the provincialisation of academic disciples such as History, Political Science, Sociology, Anthropology and etc is a Euro-American construct (Ndlovu-Gatsheni, 2018). Emerging from this, Nyawasha shows intellectual bankruptcy by conflating Afrocentricity (theory) with African studies (academic discipline). It goes without saying that Afrocentricity is one among many major theoretical perspectives in African studies and there is really no fuss about that. Emerging from the above, it is submitted that like all systems; it is in the nature of theories and academic disciplines to complement one another (Shai, 2016). The binarity that has been introduced in this realm is a by-product of the Euro-American thought system which is solely based on the cultural value systems of the Euro-Americans (Maserumule, 2011). The Euro-American cultural practices include individualism, selfishness and competition. This alien but dominant practices are at the heart of most scholars' (including Nyawasha) difficulty in acknowledging the inevitability of the complementarity of theories and academic disciplines. It is this very alien culture that makes Nyawasha to incorrectly subscribe from Ian

Hacking's fictitious conception of satiable hatred among academic colleagues who have scholarly differences. However, complementarity is well recognised in the Afrocentric thought system, which is predominantly based on the cultural values systems of the Africans. The latter set of values entail cooperation, interdependence, shared responsibility and oneness, among others.

Afrocentricity and the [De]colouring of scholarship in South Africa

Meanwhile, Nyawasha (p. 8) contradicts himself in his paper by contending "that scholarship knows no colour bar (boundary)". This observation is factually incorrect and wrongly presents scholarship as an innocent trade. Regardless of the genuine intentions of pure scholarship, the fact that this trade has been a fertile site for mischievous, under-hand and dirty mechanisations in the society cannot be easily contested. At the beginning of his paper, Nyawasha has acknowledged inequities in South African academe which #must fall campaigns exposed between the year 2015 and 2016. The same challenges can also be observed in USA and Australia. I argue that the fact that we have an African and European race does not supersede the reality of the existence of one human race as propagated by Pan Africanist Congress of Azania's (PAC) former President Robert Sobukwe. A bigger question which is beyond the scope of the current chapter is that if Africa is to be accepted as the cradle of human kind, then every human being has a cultural citizenship to Africa regardless of the extent to which some can try to delink with the mother continent. The truth of the matter is that you do not need to be Black or African to be Afrocentric (Asante, 2003). First and foremost, you need to be African conscious and Africa centred. You also need to be truly committed in all material aspects to the liberation of Africans from poverty and under-development to development and prosperity. I draw from Maserumule's (2017) editorial titled *Lies, damn lies*, in the *Journal of Public Administration*, to demonstrate the triviality of Nyawasha's (pp. 8-9) contention that "identity has a potential of undermining" intellectual rigour and other attributes of cutting edge scholarship in South Africa. Nyawasha (p. 9) seals his narrative about his qualms with identity by arguing that "there is no one single African culture or identity". I argue that Nyawasha lacks an unquestionable moral *locus standi* for an academic over-reach in terms of matters that are central to scholarship in South Africa. No one disputes that "one can still borrow from the 'western' tradition to study and examine African or Asian experiences". However, centering a Westernised angled lens to make sense of African or Asian experiences is susceptible to the commission of gross substantive transversal errors (Azibo, 2011). Nyawasha's conception of identity and culture reveals an obsession with divisions rather than the unity of Africans. The richness and diversity of African identity and culture does not in any way imply that African identity and culture do not exist. In laying this hotly contested debate to rest but in a different context, Sachs (2020: 189) submits that "Our culture, ANC [African] culture, is not a picturesque collection of separate ethnic and political cultures lined up side by side, or mixed in certain proportions; it has a real character and dynamic of its own". It is my well-considered view that things that make us (Africans) look different are far out-weighted by that which make us similar. For example, water is used in almost all African cultures to perform spiritual rituals (S. Mokgoatšana, personal communication, February 8, 2020). On the other hand, the conception and standards of the rigour of scholarship that Nyawasha fears would be spoiled by the decolonial Afrocentric turn in South Africa has never been sacrosanct by any measure and/or in any geographic space (Manyaka, 2016).

Among the plethora of mishaps in Nyawasha's paper is the wrong assumption that the Afrocentric tradition focuses only "on matters of territory and geography rather than theoretical prominence or fore-*grounding*. Grounding is one of the tenets of Afrocentricity. This bring me to conclude that among the weaknesses in Nyawasha's paper is that its author does not know what he does not know. It is such unconscious intellectual incapacity among the nemesis of Afrocentricity that forces me to re-state that Asante as cited by Modupe (2003: 62-63) conceptualised and explained three elements of the Afrocentric theoretical framework as follows:

- Grounding is the process of learning that is centred on the Africans, their, history, culture and continent.
- Orientation "is having and pursuing intellectual interest in the African and the formation of a psychological identity direction, based upon that interest, in the direction toward Africa".

- Perspective denotes self-awareness of viewing and affecting the world in a manner that prioritise the African interests and which is suggestive of the quality, kind and amount of the above mentioned two elements.

Conclusion

The recent resurgence of the decolonial Afrocentric movement exemplifies the fact that decolonisation project in South Africa and Africa as a whole remains incomplete. This should be understood within the context that inasmuch as the anti-colonial and anti-apartheid struggles were waged in South Africa, Africans were never really ready to assume power. This is because academics were marginalised during the transition period, particularly in South Africa. Such marginalisation denied them to offer intellectual resources that are crucial to the conception of alternative systems to the *isms* that troubled our society before the year 1994. Therefore, the resurgence of the decolonial Afrocentric turn in South Africa is a deliberate attempt by the Black intelligensia to reclaim their rightful place in the knowledge industry for making a meaningful contribution in pathing the futures for our country. That we (Afrocentricists) are reduced to instruments of rigidity in scholarship by merely embracing a progressive idea whose time has come for just 20 years is unfair and it is reminiscence of the application of double standards by those who are adamant in mimicking Europe as the citadel of scientific knowledge. This is because Euro-Americans have been rigid for many centuries about their monopoly of intelligence, but they hardly experienced any epistemic mutiny within their ranks.

Afrocentricity is not beyond critique, as it is the case with its Euro-American equivalents. But for one to offer an informed critique about it, you need to invest time, resources and energy to first b understand it. The pessimistic attitude and tendency expressed in Nyawasha's paper is concerning especially when it comes from an African. However, African scholars aligned to Nyawasha's line of thought can be forgiven for the commission of epistemic suicide. Such epistemic tragedy on their part is unavoidable. Hence, they have lost their cultural identity, which then presented them with glaring symptoms of epistemic confusion. The attempt to use European standards and values to measure the ability of

Afrocentricity to produce new knowledge is testament to the unevenness of global academic terrain. "Barbed wires" in scholarship in the form of gatekeeping against alternative knowledges have also been there since time immemorial. They should not be misconstrued as peculiar to South Africa.

References

Asante, M.K. 2003. Afrocentricity: *The Theory of Social Change*. Chicago: African American Images.

Asante, M.K. 2020. I Am Afrocentric and Pan-African: A Response to TawandaSydeskyNyawasha on Scholarship in South Africa. *Journal of Black Studies*.https://doi.org/10.1177/0021934720901602

Azibo, D.A. 2011. Understanding Essentialism as Fundamental: The Centred African Perspective on the Nature of Prototypical Human Nature- Cosmological Ka (Spirit).*The Western Journal of Black Studies*, 35 (2): 77-91.

Carruthers, J.H. 1999. *Intellectual Warfare*. Chicago: Third World Press.

Hussein, A. 1998. Kwame Nkrumah: Leninist Tzar or Leninist Garvey. In O.H. Kokole (ed), *The Global African: A Portrait of Ali A. Mazrui*. Trenton: Africa World Press.

Chilisa, B. 2012.*Indigenous Research Methodologies*. Los Angeles: SAGE Publications.

Landsburg, L.F. 2020.Comparative Advantage. Retrieved: https://www.econlib.org/library/Topics/Details/comparativeadvantage.html

Manyaka, R.K. 2016. Book Review- Local Government Administration in Post-Apartheid South Africa: Some Critical Perspectives, MP Sebola (Ed.). *Journal of Public Administration*, 51 (3): 436-441.

Maserumule, M.H. 2011. Good Governance in the New Partnership for Africa's Development (NEPAD: A Public Administration Perspective. Unpublished PhD Thesis. Pretoria: University of South Africa.

Maserumule, M.H. 2015. Engaged Scholarship and Liberatory Science: A Professoriate, Mount Grace, and SAAPAM in the Decoloniality Mix. *Journal of Public Administration*, 50 (2): 200-222.

Maserumule, M.H. 2017. Editorial: Lies, Damn Lies! *Journal of Public Administration*, 52 (4): 642-647.

Milam, J.H., Jr. 1992. "The Emerging Paradigm of Afrocentric Research Methods"., Paper presented at the 17th Annual Meeting of the Association for the Study of Higher Education in Minneapolis, Minnesota, 30 October 1992.

Modupe, D.S. 2003. The Afrocentric Philosophical Perspective: Narrative Outline. In Mazama, A. (Ed).*The Afrocentric Paradigm*. Trenton: Africa World Press.

Nyawasha, T. S. 2019. 'I am of Popper', 'I am of Asante': The Polemics of Scholarship in South Africa. *Studies in Philosophy and Education*, 39(1), 1–14

Reviere, R. 2001. Toward an Afrocentric research methodology. *Journal of Black Studies*, 31 (6): 709-728.

Robbins, S.P. 2016. Finding Your Voice as an Academic Writer (and Writing Clearly).*Journal of Social Work Education*, 52 (02): 133-135.

Sebola M.P. 2018. Peer review, scholarship and editors of scientific publications: the death of scientific knowledge in Africa. *KOERS-Bulletin for Christian Scholarship*, 83 (1):1-13.

Sachs, A. 2020.Preparing Ourselves for Freedom: Culture and the ANC Guidelines.Retrieved: https://www.jstor.org/stable/1146119?seq=1 #metadata_info_tab_contents.

Shai K.B. 2015.*Reader: Introduction to International Relations*. Sovenga: Turfloop Print.

Shai, K.B. 2016. An Afrocentric Critique of the United States of America's foreign policy towards Africa: The case studies of Ghana and Tanzania, 1990-2014. Unpublished PhD Thesis.Sovenga: University of Limpopo.

Shai, K.B. 2017. South African State Capture: A Symbiotic Affair between Business and State Going Bad(?) *Insight on Africa*, Vol9 (1): 62-75.

Shai, K.B. &Nyawasha, T.S. 2016. A critical appraisal of the post-Cold War United States of America's foreign policy towards Kenya: An Afrocentric perspective. *Commonwealth Youth and Development*, 14 (2): 151-169.

Shai, K.B; Nyawasha, T.S. &Ndaguba, E.A. 2018.[De] constructing South Africa's Jacob Zuma led ANC: An Afrocentric perspective. *Journal of Public Affairs*. https://doi.org/10.1002/pa.1842

Shai, K.B. 2019. The death of scientific knowledge in [South] Africa: An Afrocentric response to M.P. Sebola. *Journal of Public Affairs*, e1975. https://doi.org/10.1002/pa.1975

CHAPTER EIGHT

The Decriminalisation of the #FeesMustFall Movement in South Africa

Introduction

The year 2015 was a watershed one in South Africa's higher education landscape. In this year, the country witnessed the outbreak and mushrooming of a series of hashtag movements that were mainly led by students but supported by many people from civil society and the public and private sectors. These hashtag movements included #RhodesMustFall, #OpenStellenbosch, #TransforMWits, Black Student Movement and #FeesMustFall (Luescher 2016; Naicker 2016). Some of these movements only operated on certain university campuses (e.g. #OpenStellenbosch) whereas others' activities cut across the entire higher education landscape in South Africa (e.g. #FeesMustFall). Central to the campaigns of these movements have been grumblings in institutions of higher learning about uncertainty, violence, exploitation, and dominance of the Africans of blood by the Africans of the soil (Lushaba 2016; Mekoa 2016).

This chapter embraces Mazrui's (2004) dual typology of Africans. In South Africa, the term Africans of blood refers to the black majoritarian segment of the population. In contrast, the term Africans of the soil denotes the white minority (also known as Europeans in terms of apartheid population classification). The foregoing analysis demonstrates that while the context of the contemporary struggles of the students in South Africa is not the same as the one prior to the dawn of majority rule in the 1990s, the realities and practicalities on the ground show that the cauldron of uncertainty, violence and exploitation has stubbornly entrenched itself after the official demise of apartheid (Lushaba 2016; Phaswana 2016). It is argued that the inhumane practices of the past self-generate and renew themselves even though in the new dispensation the democratic imperatives force the advocates of these practices to operate under cover.

It seems that the present political environment in the country and the world at large leaves the perpetuation of malpractices at South African universities to naturally transit from acts of simplicity to complexity in order for them not to be easily detected by law enforcement authorities. The continuity of these practices in South Africa's universities, which resonate with Verwoerdian apartheid philosophy, shows the extent to which South African society is untransformed. The latter argument should be understood within the context of academia being the microcosm of society (Khunou 2016). Logically, if the academic environment is polluted, it means that the society where it is conceptualised is much polluted. The very meaning of the name "university" indicates that both students and staff are drawn from all corners of the country and the world; hence it can be said that the lack of adequate transformation of South African society more than 20 years after initiating majority rule in 1994 is reflected in the academic sector (Lushaba 2016).

It is on this basis that the student campaigns between 2015 and 2016 have received sympathy from the majority of the country's citizens. It is not farfetched to assert that widespread sympathy for the student campaigns is reminiscent of the anti-apartheid and colonial struggles of the masses in the 1970s and 1980s in South Africa and other parts of Southern Africa. The relevance of linking these historical and contemporary imperatives to the analysis of this discourse finds true expression in the African proverb that "the river that forgets its source will soon dry up".

To add, the renewed mass activism characterising the student campaigns, which was also a characteristic of anti-colonial and apartheid campaigns, is a direct vindication of the belief expressed in this chapter (a belief that is shared by many others) that, like other liberation movements turned ruling political parties, the African National Congress (ANC) has failed to adequately transform its liberation rhetoric into reality in respect of the higher education, labour and health sectors. Characteristically, the issues articulated by the leaders of the student campaigns between 2015 and 2016 found a fertile ground for germination through the broken moral and political contract between the political elite and the South African population.

While the calls for the student campaigns in the period under review appealed to the majority, it is worth noting that they were also perceived and embraced with reservation within certain circles. This chapter explores the #FeesMustFall movement from an Afrocentric perspective. This does not mean that other student-led hashtag movements that preceded the #FeesMustFall movement were insignificant, but the activities of the latter attracted the attention not only of domestic entities but also of the international community. Hence, the activities of the #FeesMustFall movement were to a certain extent constitutive of investment risk as their manifestations almost brought the whole of South Africa to a standstill and resulted in the concomitant shutdown of almost all institutions of higher learning in the country. While some of the genuine concerns of the #FeesMustFall campaign also appealed to those who opposed its strategy and tactics, the reality is that the discourse of this movement has been polarised.

Besides the African majority who identified themselves with the #FeesMustFall movement, there was a minority group that criminalised and demonised it due to its violent strategy and tactics. This group included the then South African Minister of Higher Education and Training, Blade Nzimande; Acting National Police Commissioner, Lieutenant General Khomotso Phahlane; ANC Secretary General, Gwede Mantashe; and the African National Congress Youth League (ANCYL) President, Collen Maine (Africa Country 2016; eNCA 2016; News24 2016; Nkwanyana 2016).

While violence as espoused by the #FeesMustFall movement may be deemed bad, it is the well-considered view of the author of this chapter that the framing of such an argument has been intentionally biased and its epistemic locus is the Euro-American paradigm, which also serves as the bedrock of South Africa's jurisprudence and academia. It is for this reason that the following section of the chapter introduces Afrocentricity as an alternative theoretical lens to decipher the discourse on the #FeesMustFall movement in South Africa.

Chapter Eight | Kgothatso B. Shai

Conceptual and Theoretical Framing: Decriminalisation vis-à-vis Afrocentricity

In the human and social sciences, conceptualising and contextualising terms is not a straightforward and conventional undertaking. This notion also applies to the conceptualisation and contextualisation of highly sensitive and politico-legally charged terms such as decriminalisation. For the purpose of this chapter, decriminalisation refers to an act of lessening penalties for certain unlawful acts (Uitermark and Cohen 2005). However, the definition of decriminalisation (the opposite of which is criminalisation) can also be extended to mean the legalisation of an act that was previously subjected to the status of criminality (Ritter 2017).

Taking a cue from the conceptualisation of the term "decriminalisation" and the competing narratives on the "fallist movement" in South Africa, foregrounding this chapter on alternative theory becomes an apparent necessity. Accordingly, this chapter is underpinned by the theory of Afrocentricity as articulated by scholars such as Asante (1990, 2003). It also draws on the works of like-minded Afrocentric scholars such as Modupe (2003), Mazama (2003), Diop (1987) and Maserumule (2015). Afrocentricity is fast emerging as an alternative theoretical tool in academia, particularly in the human and social sciences. Among the pillars of Afrocentricity is the central belief that science is not neutral but biased (Zulu 2016). In fact, what is generally accepted as scientific or science is made up of the inter-subjectivities of a certain dominant group of people. This analysis also hinges on the reality that science or epistemology is driven by a particular philosophy, and consequently its content and direction are largely shaped by the context and culture of the people who produce it (Burke 1991; Shai 2016). Ideally, such culturally and contextually conscious knowledges should reflect the cultural value systems of the communities who consume them. In relation to this, this chapter takes the stand that Africans collectively have a spectacular know-how of various aspects of life, including the global political economy (Shai 2017). Therefore, carving a safe space for sustainable conversation between the elements of Afrocentricity and other progressive ideas, concepts and theories from Africa and beyond is crucial for the production of knowledge of reality: a precursor for the realisation of amicable and irrevocable solutions to

Africa's challenges and problems (Asante 2003; Burke 1991; Gouldner 1980).

Categorically, Asante (as cited by Modupe 2003, 62–63) has conceptualised and explained three key elements of the Afrocentric theoretical framework as entailing: (1) The process of learning that is centred on Africans, their history, culture and continent; (2) The pursuit of "intellectual interest in the African and the formation of a psychological identity direction, based upon that interest, in the direction toward Africa"; and (3) self-awareness of viewing and affecting the world in a manner that prioritises African interests and that is suggestive of the quality, kind and amount of the aforementioned two elements. These three key elements of Afrocentricity are embraced and used as the analytical categories of this chapter. Asante (2003) presents them in a condensed manner whereas Modupe (2003) correctly synthesises them in a way that enriches the narrative and analytical thread of any piece of work that adopts Afrocentricity as a theoretical telescope. There is no gainsaying that Afrocentricity is relevant to this chapter because most of the academic works on the #FeesMustFall movement are purely empirical and their epistemic position is either unapologetically or unconsciously Euro-American.

As a means of contributing towards epistemic rebellion and justice, Shai's (2017, 6) Afrocentric invocation that "a blend of both empirical and non-empirical aspects produces holistic findings about [the] central questions" about any phenomena being probed, holds sway in this discourse. However, the said author's propagation "is a near impossible exercise in instances wherein the researcher limits himself to either empirical or non-empirical methods". It is within this context that this chapter wholly rejects the binary standing of knowledge as, for instance, empirical or non-empirical, evil or good, positive or negative, objective or subjective. Above all, the relevance and timeliness of the introduction of previously marginalised and silenced theories such as Afrocentricity in this chapter find expressed articulation in the African proverb that "borrowed water will not quench your thirst". It is on this ground that it is posited that if Africans are to excel in their trade (knowledge production, management and dissemination), it becomes imminently necessary for them to base their research (and chapters like this one) on

Chapter Eight | Kgothatso B. Shai

values, standards, cultures and systems that are rooted in African agency (Asante 2003).

Regardless of the coherence of Afrocentricity and the appreciation of its solid nature across the colour line, one observes that, with the exception of a few and not-so-visible scholarly insights of a few African academics, the popular public discourse on the fallist movement has been largely anti-colonial: but the strength of the white establishment has made it difficult to transit from this to a more meaningful discourse of decolonisation and Africanisation. It is the argument of this chapter that while decolonisation is a workable means for propelling the fallist movement, the goal should be "to Africanise and Africreate" in the true sense of the words. In the case of South Africa and Africa at large, there is no alternative but to Africabrate, which is about nothing else but Africanisation and pan-Africanism. This implies that the rejection of Eurocentric dominance and supremacy in the knowledge structure of the global political economy and other aspects of life by the majoritarian Africans without offering feasible alternative scholarship and other contributions would be of minimal consequence. In this context, there is no alternative to Africanisation.

The white establishment, in resisting the transformation of higher education and other societal sectors, including the economy of South Africa, finds strength and solace in the undisputed fact that "this system [coloniality] develops the intellects of the elite and political leaders and alienates their minds from the societies and peoples they are supposed to protect and represent" (Sooliman 2016, 168). In the end, the ability of the white establishment to successfully denounce transformation of the South African society, particularly its higher education sector, resonates with the co-control, ownership and management of the knowledge structure of the global political economy by the white monopoly capital which has the propensity to respond to the dictates and expectations of its international Euro-American counterparts (Shai and Iroanya 2014). While at face value the common goal of capitalists (who are mainly whites) in South Africa and beyond is to maximise profits at all costs, this chapter's position is that their key unifier is the desperate desire to maintain white dominance and supremacy in all material terms (Shai 2016).

Based on the foregoing analysis it is clear that institutions of higher learning in South Africa will change at a snail's pace "unless mind-sets start to shift" (London 2017). To add, if the class structure of South African society can be transformed, the higher education sector has the potential to follow suit. In the following section, the author of this chapter grapple with a variety of views across the spectrum that appeal to the legitimisation of the #FeesMustFall movement.

Justification for Decriminalising the #FeesMustFall Movement

There is a popular expression in political literature which says that "if you do not know where you come from, then you do not know where you are going". This expression is in sync with the juxtaposition of the troubles faced by the majoritarian Africans in South Africa and contemporaneous and historical perspectives, and of the call of the slain South African politician, Steve Biko, that "we must relate the past to the present and demonstrate evolutions of the modern black man" (Mekoa 2016, 157). In the same breath it is wrong to limit the analysis of the fallist movement to immediate conditions. A balanced view can be painted when one locates the operations of the fallist movement in historical imperatives and complements such with contemporary frames. The fertile ground for this link has also been debated by scholars such as Richard Tuck, among others. According to Tuck (1991), history is the study of the politics of the past while politics is the study of the history of the present.

Flowing from the above, one notes that the anti-apartheid colonialism rhetoric as espoused by various liberation movements-cum-ruling political parties, such as the ANC in South Africa, SWAPO in Namibia and the Popular Movement for the Liberation of Angola (MPLA), was embedded in unfulfilled promises for decent jobs, better education and health care after independence or in the new dispensation (Khapoya 2010). In South Africa, for instance, the Freedom Charter (Congress of the People 1955), which has served as a political instrument and moral contract between the ANC-led Congress Alliance (including the Communist Party of South Africa and other structures not mentioned here) and the previously oppressed African masses and other marginalised groups, it is unequivocally stated that "The doors of learning and culture shall be opened" to all. It is further stated that

> Education shall be free, compulsory, universal and equal for all children; Higher education and technical training shall be opened to all by means of state allowances and scholarships awarded on the basis of merit" (Congress of the People 1955, 3).

In analysing the statement that "Education shall be free", the Education Policy Consortium (2015) maintains the official ANC-led Government narrative that such a clause did not include higher education and training. This clause was also not explicit in terms of its interpretation, and its reference was therefore limited to basic education. Thus, it is safe to argue that the official narrative (propaganda) of the Government as confirmed by the Education Policy Consortium is driven by nothing else but the desperate desire to qualify the incompetence of the political elite in effectively handling challenges relating to the funding of the higher education sector in South Africa (Isike and Ogunnubi 2017; Mbeki and Mbeki 2016; Sebola and Tsheola 2015).

If one is to critically reflect on the open letter penned by Lushaba (2016) and numerous statements attributed to the leaders of the fallist movement, it becomes apparent that while the ANC has had reasonable achievements in respect of the massification of universities, the truth of the matter is that it has not been able to efficiently alter the colonial/apartheid patterns of higher education. Quality education is still a privilege for minority whites and a few children from black elite families. The payment model of historically white universities, such as the universities of Cape Town and the Witwatersrand, naturally excludes children from financially disadvantaged families to access their facilities. They charge unreasonable and exorbitant fees for tuition, accommodation and other related services. In addition to the fact that the composition of student and staff population is still largely white, the foregoing assertion partly explains the reason why historically white universities were the biggest targets of the #FeesMustFall campaign. While the private sector and the Government provide bursaries, and loans are channelled through the National Student Financial Aid Scheme (NSFAS), these have the propensity of leaving many students trapped in debt due to increasing levels of unemployment in South Africa. Some of these challenges are not specific to South Africa and can also be observed in other African countries with a colonial history. The curriculum in almost all South African universities does not reflect the values and aspirations of the majority of this country. The staff complement (particularly at a senior level) in some universities (e.g. the University of Pretoria and Stellenbosch University) does not reflect the realities of population dynamics in South Africa. This is by no means an accident: it was a well-orchestrated plan by the white establishment to ensure that the negative effect of apartheid/colonialism on the majority of Africans is stubbornly perpetuated even long after apartheid has officially ended.

In the post-1994 era, the promise of a free and quality higher education has been given legislative and political effect through the incorporation of more or less similar calls in the Reconstruction and Development (RDP) strategy and the resolutions of ANC elective congresses; the one in Polokwane (Limpopo province) in 2007 (ANC 2007) and the other in Mangaung (Free State province) in 2012 (ANC 2012). As the macro-policy framework, the RDP sought to position South Africa as the hub of economic development in Southern Africa and Africa at large (Shai 2009). If Nelson Mandela's assertion that "Education is the most powerful weapon which you can use to change the world" is anything to go by, it is sensible to recognise that there is no way in which South Africa can drive the process of sustainable socio-economic development if its higher education sector is in peril, largely being reminiscent of the posture of Bantu education (Nkuna and Shai 2016). It is also in the spirit and letter of section 29 and subsection 1(b) of the Constitution of the Republic of South Africa, 1996 that "Everyone has the right to further education, which the state, through reasonable measures, must make progressively available and accessible". Regardless of this, there are some within government circles who have reservations about South Africa's desirability for and affordability of free higher education (Parker 2015). They advance economic reasons to qualify their claim that the calls for quality free education as advocated by the fallist movement are unreasonable and therefore not in sync with what lawmakers had in mind when they conceptualised section 29 and subsection 1(b) of the Constitution. This argument is contested by some in certain circles who cite developing countries such as Cuba, Botswana and Burundi as success stories for the provision of free and quality education. Taking cognisance of the malaise of political constraints, such as the Nkandla debacle, the state capture saga and the prevalence of shoddy Black Economic Empowerment (BEE) deals, these naturally neutralise and invalidate the case against providing quality and free higher education in South Africa on the basis of simple cost analyses (Isike and Ogunnubi 2017).

While the author of this chapter identify themselves with the case for the provision of quality higher education on the basis of historical, political, moral and humanitarian grounds, it is also their view that it is good to benchmark with other developing countries such as Cuba when confronting challenges pertaining to retarded levels of the transformation of higher education in South Africa. However, it is also important to contextualise the lessons drawn (Sizani 2016) as the political and socio-economic calculus of South Africa is not necessarily the same as that of other developing countries that may be providing free and quality education to their citizens.

It is emphasised that, at a political party level, the case for the #FeesMustFall campaign has also had a qualitative effect. For example, the ANC resolved during its 2007 elective conference to "progressively introduce free education for the poor until undergraduate level" and it undertook "to focus on the quality of education" in South Africa (ANC 2007). These are the two critical clauses constituting the Polokwane conference's ANC resolutions that have relevance to higher education and to the focus of this chapter. Five years down the line, the ANC resolved at the Mangaung conference in 2012 that "The policy for free higher education to all undergraduate level students will be finalised for adoption before the end of 2013" (ANC 2012).

The focus on the ANC at the expense of other political parties in discoursing about higher education transformation in South Africa should be understood within the context that this party is not only ruling the country but is dominating its political landscape. It is on this basis that in the case of South Africa, in contrast to the theory of governance, the reality is that there is no watertight separation between the state and the ruling party. What can be deduced from the foregoing analysis is that there seems to be the political goodwill on the part of the ANC-led Government to provide free and quality education, but the global pressures of the dominant neo-liberal order are not making it easy (Bond 2007; Shai and Iroanya 2014). As a result, the political and governmental efforts to translate what appear to be good postulations on higher education into meaningful actions are usurped by capitalist global forces. In addition, Mbeki and Mbeki (2016, 103) attribute the failure of the ruling elite to deliver free and quality education to all, in particular higher education and training, to such delivery hinging on "hostility toward the welfare of the worker". The said authors add that "the ruling elite is anti-education as it sees this as a threat".

Case against the #FeesMustFall Campaign

In contrast to the case for the #FeesMustFall, there is also a counter-thesis that is not so strong. The arguments against the #FeesMustFall movement are rooted within the ANC, Government, student bodies, civil society and beyond. It is interesting that at a certain point, especially towards the end of 2016, some of the people who had supported the #FeesMustFall movement earlier swiftly joined the bandwagon of those who renounced some of its activities. The latter group was not necessarily for the criminalisation of the fallist movement but against some of the elements of its modus operandi. Public violence, arson, intimidation, character assassination, malicious damage to both private and public property and the disturbance of public order were some of the manifestations that later characterised the fallist movement. Table 1 below provides details of the costs of damage at affected universities as a result of student protests based on preliminary assessments as of 15 March 2016 as reported by the Ministry of Higher Education and Training (Nkwanyana 2016). According to Nkwanyana, the estimated costs are based on reported incidents of campus unrest for the period October 2015 to January 2016 (see Table 1).

Table 1: Estimated cost of damage relating to campus unrest: October 2015–January 2016

Institution	Estimated cost of damage
University of Stellenbosch	R352 000.00
North West University	R612 000.00
University of Limpopo	R1 786 294.52
University of Johannesburg	R345 000.00
University of the Western Cape	R46 544 446.00
Walter Sisulu University	R351 287.19
Tshwane University of Technology	R5 073 747.73
University of KwaZulu-Natal	R82 000 000.00
Cape Peninsula University of Technology	R689 850.14
University of Cape Town	R1 415 693.14
University of Zululand	R4 500 000.00
Rhodes University	R250 000.00
University of the Witwatersrand	R1 410 223.00
Total	**R145 330 541.72**

Source: Nkwanyana 2016

The extent of the devastation, as indicated in Table 1, provided fertile ground for the criminalisation of the fallist movement by the judiciary, the security establishment, politicians, court of public opinion and other interested parties. The position of the security establishment has been that the fallist movement has been infiltrated by a third force for reasons that are not related to the genuine cause of the movement, reasons that have never been divulged by the state security apparatus. The theory of the third force within the fallist movement is shared by Maine and Mantashe (as cited in Sooliman 2016) who believe that the campaign was penetrated by bad elements who sought to use it as a platform to engineer regime change in South Africa. This narrative has germinated seeds of political, ideological, class, gender and colour divisions within the fallist movement, which have achieved nothing except to weaken the #FeesMustFall campaign. The reality that various dimensions of the #FeesMustFall movement are fragmented and that its pioneers are not permanent students renders its sustainability in doubt.

The foregoing narrative is in sync with South Africa's political climate at the time, which witnessed repeated calls from within and outside the ANC for President Jacob Zuma to step down as the head of State and Government following widespread revelations that he had breached his oath of office (Mogoeng 2016). The judiciary's central focus on the activities of the fallist movement has been its criminal dimension. It is generally believed in legal circles that there is no sound basis to use violence to achieve certain ends, including but not limited to the transformation of higher education in South Africa. Hence, the new democratic dispensation has unveiled numerous legal mechanisms for registering one's concerns, grievances, challenges and problems regarding any issue in society. The author of this chapter contend that ubuntu/botho and other African cultural value systems are often missing in the interpretation of the law statutes of this country. This situation is the by-product of the reality that the development of legislative bodies in South Africa has been heavily influenced by and immersed in Roman-Dutch Law to the detriment of the indigenous legal system.

Furthermore, others argue that inasmuch as students have a just struggle to wage, it should never be at the expense of the safety and security of others and of private and public property. What seems to be missing from the dominant discourse on the fallist movement is the lack of appreciation of the extent to which factional politics has contributed to the escalation of this campaign to uncontrollable levels and violent proportions. As cited by Kubayi (2016), Oliver Tambo, the exiled president of the ANC, in 1977 counselled his comrades in Angola as follows:

> You might think it is very difficult to wage a liberation struggle. Wait until you are in power. I might be dead by then. At that stage you will realize that it is actually more difficult to keep power than to wage a liberation war. People will be expecting a lot of services from you. You will have to satisfy the various demands of the masses of our people. In the process, be prepared to learn from other people's revolutions. Learn from the enemy also. The enemy is not necessarily doing everything wrongly. You may take his right tactics and use them to your advantage. At the same time, avoid repeating the enemy's mistakes.

The above words attributed to Tambo represent an oasis of wisdom and in fact it is not farfetched to say they were prophetic of what is currently happening in the ANC and South Africa. Prior to 1994, successive National Party (NP) regimes that presided over white minority rule in South Africa criminalised and demonised the forces opposed to their segregationist policies, branding these as terrorists or murderers. These labels were often pinned to cadres of the liberation movements such as the ANC, the Communist Party of South Africa (CPSA), the Pan Africanist Congress of Azania (PAC) and the Azanian People's Organisation (AZAPO). Such labelling and framing were exploited by the NP's propagandists to shape public opinion in South Africa and beyond towards their favour. If the NP Government was able to vilify the pioneers of liberation in South Africa to entrench its apartheid rule, and assuming that Tambo's counsel was well-considered and received by his comrades, it can be argued that the ANC is using the very same strategy to disparage the fallist movement and any tentacle that is seen to be constituting a threat to its rule.

While the possibility of the infiltration of the third force in the fallist movement cannot be wholly dismissed, this author' contention is that such allegations have been deliberately blown out of proportion by the ANC for the purpose of shifting the focus from the genuine struggles of the students, their supporters and sympathisers. The chaos theory points out that wanton violence against an unethical system and all its manifestations can be ethical depending on the standard of measure used (Nabudere 2012, 40).

It is also important to appreciate that other push and pull factors may be propelling the fallist movement to engage in criminal activities. Among other things, the violence engulfing South Africa's universities explains the violent culture of this country which dates back to the heydays of the anti-apartheid struggle (Shai and Mothibi 2015). Also leaning on the counsel of Tambo, one appreciates the fact that violence was one of the means the ANC and other liberation movements used to fight and defeat apartheid. As such, it makes sense for the fallist movement (which includes members of the ANC) to regard public assets as soft targets for getting the ANC-led Government to adequately and with a sense of urgency attend to the plight of the majoritarian Africans in South African universities.

One of the key lessons that can be learnt from the protests (e.g. the recent one in Malamulele) and campaigns (e.g. the fallist one) across the country is that violence has become one of the most efficient ways to communicate with the ANC-led Government. In fact, violence appears to be the language that the ANC-led Government understands best (Nkuna and Shai 2016). Even if there are a few bad elements in the fallist movement who engage in criminal activities, it is factually wrong to attach negative connotations to the entire campaign. Contextually, the combination of the narratives that blatantly criminalise the fallist movement is well captured by Sooliman (2016, 168) when he avers that whiteness is the only mode of description and analysis that captures the essence of the reflections on "the statements by Gwede Mantashe and Blade Nzimande during the months of September 2016 in response to the student protests".

Conclusion

As has been established and indicated in this chapter, the #FeesMustFall campaign started at the University of the Witwatersrand but it soon became a national issue. Political and economic instability is the common denominator of the political landscape of South Africa and also of many countries in Africa. As such it is politically, morally and historically correct for the fallist movement to demand quality and free higher education, although a decision to meet this demand might not be economically sound in respect of the immediate future.

The transformation of the higher education sector and the provision of quality and free high education should be the long-term goal of the South African society as a whole and it should not be the only focus of the Government. The tendency of the Government is to create a lot of problems when resolving a single problem. While it is fashionable to talk about quality, decolonisation and free education in the public space, the theoretical framework of this chapter is Afrocentricity, and in line with that it is proposed that a transition needs to be made from decolonised to Africanised discourse. There could be success stories in Africa and elsewhere in respect of the provision of free and quality higher education, but a one-size-fits-all approach that disregards the unique conditions of a country cannot hold water.

The fallist movement's call for the provision of free and quality higher education enjoys sympathy at both government and political party levels in South Africa, and its envisaged value for the entire society is indicative of the fact that the narrative regarding its criminalisation cannot be sustained. This chapter posits that the experiences of the student protests in South Africa between the years 2015 and 2016 problematise the perception that this country has good policies. It is concluded that the only time to know if a country has a good policy is when such a policy has been implemented.

References

Africa Country. 2016. "UWC Fees Will Fall Movement Intelligence Report Part 1. Free Education Now or Never!" Accessed March 21, 2016. http://africasacountry.org/posted_docs/Student_Rebellion_Counter_Narrative%20UWC_21_March_2016.pdf.

ANC (African National Congress). 2007. "52nd National Conference: Resolutions." Accessed December 20, 2016. http://www.anc.org.za/content/52nd-national-conference-resolutions.

ANC (African National Congress). 2012. "53rd National Conference Resolutions." Accessed April 14, 2013. http://www.anc.org.za/docs/res/2013/resolutions53r.pdf.

Asante, M. K. 1990. *Kemet, Afrocentricity and Knowledge*. Trenton, NJ: Africa World Press.

Asante, M. K. 2003. *Afrocentricity: The Theory of Social Change*. Chicago, IL: African American Images.

Bond, P. 2007. "South Africa between Neoliberalism and Social Democracy?: Respecting Balance While Sharpening Differences." *Politikon: South African Journal of Political Studies* 34 (2): 125–46. https://doi.org/10.1080/02589340701715182.

Burke, P., ed. 1991. *New Perspectives on Historical Writing*. Cambridge: Polity Press. Congress of the People. 1955. *The Freedom Charter*. London: ANC. Constitution of the Republic of South Africa. 1996.

Diop, C. A. 1987. Pre-Colonial Black Africa: A Comparative Study of the Political and Social Systems of Europe and Black Africa, from Antiquity to the Formation of Modern States. Westport, CT: Lawrence Hilland.

Education Policy Consortium. 2015. *Education and the Freedom Charter: A Critical Appraisal*. EPC Occasional Paper 5. Accessed October 7,

2016. http://www.dhet.gov.za/ResearchNew/18.%20EPC%20Occasional%20Paper%205%20-%20Education%20and%20the%20Freedom%20Charter,%20A%20critical%20appraisal.pdf.

eNCA. 2016. "Third Force at Work in #FeesMustFall: Phahlane." Accessed October 7, 2016. https://www.enca.com/south-africa/third-force-at-work-in-feesmustfall-phahlane.

Gouldner, A. W. 1980. *The Two Marxisms: Contradictions and Anomalies in the Development Theory.* London: MacMillan. https://doi.org/10.1007/978-1-349-16296-3.

Isike, C., and O. Ogunnubi. 2017. "The Discordant Soft Power Tunes of South Africa's Withdrawal from the ICC." *Politikon: South African Journal of Political Studies* 44 (1): 173–79. https://doi.org/10.1080/02589346.2017.1274085.

Khapoya, V. B. 2010. *The African Experience: An Introduction.* New York, NY: Longman.

Khunou, G. 2016. "Writing to Stay: Running Shoes Replaced with High Heels." Paper delivered at the University of Limpopo's Dialogue Day on What Does it Mean to be Black in the South African Academy, Sovenga, University of Limpopo, April 22, 2016.

Kubayi, N. 2016. "Oliver Tambo's Quote". Facebook, August 15, 2016. https://www.facebook.com/bishopoliver.tambo.

London, T. 2017. "South African Universities Won't Change Unless Mind-Sets Start to Shift." The Conversation. Accessed January 11, 2017. http://www.polity.org.za/article/south-african-universities-wont-change-unless-mindsets-start-to-shift-2017-01-11.

Luescher, T. 2016. "Towards an Intellectual Engagement with the #Student Movements in South Africa." *Politikon: South African Journal of Political Studies* 43 (1): 145-48. https://doi.org/10.1080/02589346.2016.1155138.

Lushaba, L. S. 2016. An Open Letter to Professor Anthony Butler, HOD: Department of Political Studies, University of Cape Town, August 30, 2016.

Maserumule, M. H. 2015. "Engaged Scholarship and Liberatory Science: A Professoriate, Mount Grace, and SAAPAM in the Decoloniality Mix." *Journal of Public Administration* 50 (2): 200–222.

Mazama, A., ed. 2003. *The Afrocentric Paradigm*. Trenton, NJ: Africa World Press.

Mazrui, A. A. 2004. The African Predicament and the American Experience: A Tale of Two Edens. London: Praeger.

Mbeki, M., and N. Mbeki. 2016. *A Manifesto for Social Change: How to Save Africa*. Johannesburg: Picador Africa.

Mekoa, I. 2016. Silent No More: Challenges Facing Black African Academics at South African Universities. Cape Town: Incwadi.

Modupe, D. S. 2003. "The Afrocentric Philosophical Perspective: A Narrative Outline." In *The Afrocentric Paradigm*, edited by A. Mazama, 55–72. Trenton, NJ: Africa World Press.

Mogoeng, M. 2016. Economic Freedom Fighters v Speaker of the National Assembly and Others; Democratic Alliance v Speaker of the National Assembly and Others [2016] ZACC 11. Judgement. Braamfontein: Constitutional Court of South Africa.

Nabudere, D. W. 2012. *Afrikology and Transdisciplinarity: A Restorative Epistemology*. Pretoria: Africa Institute of South Africa (AISA).

Naicker, C. 2016. "From Marikana to #FeesMustFall: The Praxis of Popular Politics in South Africa." *Urbanisation* 1 (1): 53–61. https://doi.org/10.1177%2F2455747116640434.

News24. 2016. "Third Force or ANC Paranoia? Mantashe on fees flights." Accessed September 27, 2016. http://www.news24.com/Video/SouthAfrica/News/third-force-or-anc-paranoia-mantashe-on-fees-fights-20160927.

Nkuna V. M., and K. B. Shai. 2016. "An Exploration of the 2016 Violent Protests with Specific Reference to Vuwani Community in Limpopo Province." Paper presented at the 5th Annual South African Association of Public Administration and Management (SAAPAM) Conference—Limpopo Chapter, The Park (Mokopane), South Africa, October 26-28, 2016.

Nkwanyana, K. 2016. "On the Cost of Damage in Our Universities Arising from 2015 Students Protests." Ministry of Higher Education and Training. Statement. March 15, 2016. Pretoria: Department of Higher Education and Training.

Parker, D. 2015. "What does 'free education for all' really mean?" Accessed November 1, 2016. http://www.dhet.gov.za/SiteAssets/Latest%20News/Independent%20Thinking%20Second%20Edition/dhetpage3.pdf.

Phaswana, E. 2016. "The Limits of Being and Knowledge in the Academy." Paper delivered at the Limpopo University' s' Dialogue Day on What Does it Mean to be Black in the South African Academy, Sovenga, University of Limpopo, April 22, 2016.

Ritter, A. 2017. "Decriminalisation or legalisation: Injecting Evidence in the Drug Law Reform Debate." Accessed January 9, 2017. https://ndarc.med.unsw.edu.au/blog/decriminalisation-or-legalisation-injecting-evidence-drug-law-reform-debate.

Sebola M. P., and J. Tsheola. 2015. "African Societies, Nation-States, Governance, Human Migration, Xenophobia and Cultural Contestations: Editorial Framing." *Journal for Transdisciplinary Research in Southern Africa* 11 (4): iii–x.

Shai, K. B. 2009. *Rethinking United States-South Africa Relations.* Hoedspruit: Royal Batubatse Foundation.

Shai, K. B. 2016. "An Afrocentric Critique of the United States of America's Foreign Policy towards Africa: The Case Studies of Ghana and Tanzania, 1990–2014." PhD thesis, University of Limpopo, South Africa.

Shai, K. B. 2017. "South African State Capture: A Symbiotic Affair between Business and State Going Bad (?)". *Insight on Africa,* Vol 9 (1): 1–14. https://doi.org/10.1177/0975087816674584.

Shai, K. B., and R. O. Iroanya. 2014. "A Critical Appraisal of the American Ideological Position on Africa's Democratisation." *Journal of Public Administration* 49 (3): 909–23.

Shai, K. B., and K. A. Mothibi. 2015. "Describing pre-2009 Xenophobic Violence in South Africa: A Human Right Perspective." In *African Governance: Society, Human Migration, State, Xenophobia and Business Contestations,* edited by M. P. Sebola, J. P. Tsheola, and M. J. Mafunisa. Proceedings of the 4th SAAPAM Annual Conference—Limpopo Chapter, Polokwane, South Africa, October 28–30, 2015.

Sizani, R. K. 2016. "Keynote Address" delivered on the occasion of the 16th Annual South African Association of Public Administration and Management (SAAPAM) Conference, International Convention Centre, East London, South Africa, May 2–4, 2016.

Sooliman, Q. S. 2016. "Review of *#RhodesMustFall: Nibbling at Resilient Colonialism in South Africa* by Francis B. Nyamnjoh." *Strategic Review for Southern Africa* 38 (2): 167–69.

Tuck, R. 1991. "History of Political Thought." In *New Perspectives on Historical Writing*, edited by P. Burke, 193–205. Oxford: Blackwell.

Uitermark, J., and P. Cohen. 2005. *Encyclopedia of Law and Society*. s.v. "Decriminalisation: A Short Description, and the Social Process behind It." London: Sage Publications.

Zulu, Z. 2016. "Messages and Testimonials from IKS Practitioners and Entrepreneurs." Paper delivered at the 6th African Unity for Renaissance (AUR) Conference hosted by the Thabo Mbeki African Leadership Institute (TMALI), Pretoria, May 23–25, 2016.

CHAPTER NINE

Examining the Deficit of Youth Leadership in South Africa: An Afrocentric Student Perspective

Introduction

Globally, youth constitute a large portion of most countries and regions. In Africa, it is estimated that 65% of its 1.1 billion populace is under the age of 35 (African Youth and Governance Conference Initiative, 2015). In South Africa, Tracey (2016) notes that during the first Independent Electoral Commission of South Africa's (IEC) voter registration weekend for the 2016 Municipal elections, young people under the age of 30 accounted "for as much as 78.6% of new registrations". This positive development on South Africa's political landscape is something that political parties and observers cannot afford to overlook. It also reignites the interest on youth matters by both politicians and scholars following the #fees must fall campaign across the entire sector of South Africa's higher education since the last quarter of the year 2015 (Buys, 2016; Mancu, 2016; National Education, Health and Allied Workers Union, NEHAWU 2016).

The impressive registration of youth during the IEC's March 2016 registration drive is a departure from the general voter apathy among youth ranks and South Africans at large (Kivilu, Davids, Langa, Maphunye, Mncwango, Sedumedi & Struwig, 2005; Shultz-Herzenberg, 2014). That is to say that since the second democratic and inclusive elections in 1999, the number of South Africans and youth in particular, with an interest in electoral matters has dwindled. This dwindling in terms of the total number of potential voters and votes among the youth category is concerning especially if one is to consider that vote franchise is a right that Africans have been deprived from exercising before the dawn of democracy in the early 1990s. It is also worrisome if one is to consider that many people have sacrificed their lives so that South Africans across the colour, aged 18 and above could afford an opportunity to vote for their government (Shai, 2009). One of the dominant narratives of voter apathy among the youth has been that most of them (current crop) have not experienced the wrath of the inhumane and evil system of apartheid. Hence, it is not surprising that to a reasonable extent; they do not appreciate some of the opportunities availed by the new democratic dispensation. These opportunities include the right to vote. No matter the merits and demerits of the youths' disinterestedness on electoral matters in the recent past; it is the well-considered view of this chapter that the dominant narrative highlighted above only offers a partial guide to understanding the changing voting patterns and culture of South Africans. It is argued that the renewed interest of the youth on electoral matters can be understood within the context that issues directly affecting them (i.e. education) are dominating the agenda of the present public and political discourse in South Africa (Mancu, 2016; NEHAWU, 2016).

From the developments at the local, continental and international level, there is no gainsaying that the wave of democratisation has presented both challenges and opportunities for the youth in South Africa, Africa and the world at large. Some of these challenges are new and others are historical, but they represent themselves with modern features. As such, different countries have identified various months for bemoaning challenges faced by youth and for celebrating the opportunities enjoyed by the youth. For instance, in the Caribbean islands, February is considered as a special month in the political calendar of Cuba. Thus, it is in this month in 1959 that Cuba's revolutionary leader Fidel Castro became the country's youngest ever Prime Minister *cum* President (Thaba, 2016). This milestone has served as an inspiration, courage and a lesson that young people also have a 'transformist' role in their countries. In South Africa, June is generally regarded as the youth month. It was in this month during in 1976 that students in Soweto and South Africa at large; waged wide range campaigns rejecting Afrikaans as a medium of instruction in teaching and learning (Vuma, 2013).

Some of the post-1994 prominent leaders in South Africa belong to the "1976 generation of students". Considering this, it is befitting to argue that their elevation into the political and government circles of the democratic state has also carried hopes for the expression of the interests, aspirations and frustrations of the youth. Although the political, material and socio-economic conditions of Cuba and South Africa differ; the two countries have a lot of lessons to learn from each other, because both nations are developing countries.

Against this background, this chapter employs the triangulation of Afrocentric and qualitative research methods to: (1) determine the extent to which student movements influence party politics (2) establish the role of students in the various activities of their allied-political parties. It is emphasised that the epistemic location of this chapter is the Afrocentric paradigm as articulated by scholars such as Asante (2003) and Modupe (2003), *inter alia*.

Analytical framework

To provide a definition to the key concepts related to the topical question under consideration: (1) Student movements and (2) youth; it is observable that the definition of concepts in humanities and social sciences, in particular, is always a contested issue among academics, practitioners, analysts and commentators (Shai, 2013: 91). For this chapter, student movements refer to the organised networks of learners and/ or students that agitate for political, economic and socio-cultural change at both the basic and/or tertiary educational landscape. While the term 'student movements' is generally tied to student formations at institutions of higher learning, it is worth noting that their struggles are traditionally waged around issues of student funding, accommodation and curriculum development (Vuma, 2013).

On the other hand, 'youth' denotes young people in the age range of 14 and 35 years. These young people are found inside and outside the formal school system. Since university student political activists are also members of the society, it is notable that the membership of student movements and youth organisations outside the education sector overlap one another. This development has also meant that student grievances also include unemployment, limited business opportunities, substance abuse, poverty, inequality and retarded levels of socio-economic development. This shows the difficulty in perceiving the youth as constituting a homogenous category. Contextually, an overlap in terms of the membership and challenges of both student movements and broad youth formations makes it difficult to separate them (National Youth Commission, 2002). To compound matters to an already worse situation, a trend is currently emerging on South Africa's political landscape wherein wider youth organisations including those of the African National Congress (ANC) and Economic Freedom Fighters (EFF) contest Student Representative Council (SRC) elections at tertiary institutions of learning. This precedent means that these formations have assumed the dual identity, both as youth movements and student movements.

Afrocentric paradigm and analysis of qualitative data

In this chapter, a clear distinction between the theory of Afrocentricity and Afrocentric research methodology is drawn. While this chapter is located within the qualitative research methodology and it employed the Afrocentric research methodology as it enables in-depth and detailed analyses within the context of a limited number of persons, it reduces the potential generalisation of the findings (Mafisa&Mtati, 2009: 7). However, this chapter is critical of the mainstream research paradigms in social sciences due to their location within the Western world view. Inasmuch as the Afrocentric paradigm is generally considered as a re-enforcer of qualitative research methodology, it is introduced in this chapter as an alternative to the dominant research paradigms, which are largely rooted within a Euro-American world view (interview, University of Limpopo's Psychology Professor, 13 February 2015). The competing narratives about the dominance and location of mainstream research paradigms is well-captured by Scheurich and Young (1997: 9) who correctly assert that "dominant epistemologies are a product of White social history". Nonetheless, the Afrocentric research methodology and qualitative research methodology have shared characteristics in that both of them "assume that people employ interpretive schemes which must be understood and that the character of the local context must be articulated" (Mkabela, 2005: 188; Owusu-Ansah & Mji, 2013: 3). The foregoing argument is backed up by Mkabela (2005) who notes that the principles underpinning the Afrocentric research methodology and qualitative research methodology are common. However, the Afrocentric research methodology is driven by the ideals, interests and needs of Africa and people of African descent across the globe; but it is colour blind (Asante, 1990; Welsing, 2015). In this context, this chapter largely relied on document analysis. This was complemented with interview data. The latter was generated through semi-structured interviews with 6 respondents, who were purposively selected from youth leaders and academics at the universities of Limpopo and Venda. It is important to note that for this study, written and spoken text were not analysed separately because they are considered as complimenting each other and the possibility of treating and classifying them as mutually exclusive is dismissed (interview, University of Limpopo's History Lecturer, 12 February 2015).

Bridging the gap between policy theory and practice in party politics

In South Africa, students at both high school level and universities have been instrumental in deepening the struggle against the evil, inhumane and brutal system of apartheid. For example, historical and political archives have it on good record that the 1976 Soweto Uprising was led by high school students. Furthermore, according to the State of the Youth Report (2002: 3) "what started as student movement in 1969 with the formation of the South African Students Organisation (SASO) became a wider national youth movement against the hostile economic, social, political and educational conditions imposed by the apartheid system". Contextually, the 1976 generation that led the Soweto Uprising were influenced by the revolutionary theory and ideology of SASO and other liberation movements with cells or hide-nests in institutions of higher learning including then University College of the North (Badat, 1999). Linked to the discourse on institutions of high learning as the site of the struggle against apartheid, the University College of the North (now University of Limpopo) has produced and/or nurtured liberation pioneers such as Onkgopotse Abraham Tiro, Peter Mokaba, Cyril Ramaphosa, Barney Pityana, Mosiuoa "Terror" Lekota, PandelaniNefolovhodwe and many others.

Given the prominent role of student movements in the struggle against apartheid, it is legitimate to expect political parties to consider youth representation in their candidate lists for municipal, provincial and national elections in the new democratic dispensation. However, age should not be the only criterion for this selection or nomination. Issues of political maturity, mental capacity and capability to engage with the policy discourse of the day must be used as a point of departure. The legitimate expectation to have youth representatives in candidate lists can be well and appropriately justified by the continual existence and relevance of student movements in the new South Africa. Hence, student activists are generally considered as the sub-category of intellectuals (Mashayekhi, 2001). To this end, the intellectual orientation of the student activists puts them at the edge of leading the urgent task (at least theoretically) for the South African nation to embark on a National Programme of Political Literacy. Closely related to this, Nkondo (2012:18) observes that "political literacy constitutes the only sure avenue of opportunity to build a responsible citizenry, the only way of combating most of the heated but blind debates that now condemn South Africans to anxiety, astonishment and bewilderment". In the same breath, this political discourse was advanced by the former President Thabo Mbeki. While addressing African student leaders at the University of Cape Town in September 2010, he strongly opined that "Like the rest of the African masses, I am convinced that you, our student leaders and the students you lead, will not disappoint our expectation that you will use your considerable capacity as young African intellectuals both to comprehend and educate us about our African past and contemporary reality, to better empower us to understand what we need to do today and tomorrow(Mbeki, 2010:10)." The dichotomy between Nkondo and Mbeki's convictions is testimony to the gigantic task lying ahead of the student movements and youth in general in terms of the reconstruction and development of South Africa.

Despite this, this chapter advances that the youth are included in these lists simply because they have proved to be 'a special category of the voting population' in South Africa. This category (youth) can swing votes to go either way. Viewing the youth as 'vote-swingers' speaks to why they are often included in political party lists. Young voters can simply vote a certain political party upon knowing that one of their own has been included on the party list. In contradistinction, in some cases, the youth are used to fight factional battles within political parties (Intra-ANC; intra Cope, Intra EFF etc.) where they are included in election lists to diffuse or dilute these intra-party tensions or factional fights (interview, University of Limpopo's Sociology Lecturer, 14 February 2015).

Sadly, the prevailing cultural conditions in South Africa have produced a dominant mode of politics which does not have respect for principle and intellectualism (interview, University of Venda's History Lecturer, 13 February 2015). It is not uncommon to hear South African politicians in private alluding that 'you can't eat a principle or morality'. Such narrow arguments have been politically and historically justified by others who proclaimed in public that they did not 'join the struggle to be poor' (Mpumelelo, 2011). This moral dilemma should be understood within the context of Ramose's (2002) thesis that Ubuntu is the root of

African culture. However, emerging trends in the practice of politics in Africa and South Africa in particular show that money and material benefits have eroded the humanist essence of African culture (Ramose, 2002). This is a situation that makes it difficult for student movements to successfully agitate for the inclusion of development-driven young people in the candidate lists of political parties. This point was equally and succinctly captured by Isaak (1985: 272) when he lamented that "When a society values economic activities above all else, business leaders gain control". This is an unfortunate situation that entrenches the dominant mode of politics which is in a crisis and ought to be transformed, as a matter of urgency, if the democracy of South Africa is to be sustainable (Djanie, 2016).

It is for this reason that the envisaged generational mix of political parties' candidate lists is often invisible at certain levels of political contestation and not clear in others. This can be partly attributed to the fact that organisational interests are often sacrificed in favour of personal interests. Clientelism, patronage and *rent-seeking* have become the vices of modern politics. In most cases, votes are used in exchange for jobs, positions etc (Nyawasha, 2015). In relation to this, one former student leader retorts that:

> Students have always played a pivotal role in mobilising support for their mother bodies. Pan Africanist Congress of Azania (PAC) have the only one strongest and vibrant structure which is the Pan Africanist Student Movement of Azania (PASMA). It relies on us for support. We have always fought for representation in the party. Our National PASMA president is the ex officio of the PAC NEC and this allows us to be represented well. In the party list to the IEC, we elect at least five people from the youth ranks to be in the top twenty. Unfortunately, we have not had any young person in parliament as a result of the party's dismal electoral performance. There is also an internal democracy in the party wherein young leaders compete to be in the list and branches (including campus-based special branches) demonstrate support to their favourite candidate(s). This has again caused many problems for the PAC whereby the student movement is occasionally used to fight mother body's internal strife. We are then promised top positions or funding for personal or branch survival in return (interview, PAC leader, 14 February 2015).

Conversely, it is also safe to argue that it is common practice within the South African political terrain for delegates (including those from student movements) to be given a particular mandate by off-campus leaders to vote in a certain manner, which may not be necessarily be in the best interest of credible and fair representation of youth in the candidate lists of their respective parties. Ironically, such behind-the-scenes manipulation of voting during lists conference of various political parties are often characterised by total disregard for leadership credentials and experience in favour of attributes ranging from trustworthiness, solidarity and loyalty. Equally important, student activists are often bought with money, alcohol, promise of jobs and other material benefits to suppress the emergence of genuine representatives of the youth on the candidate lists of various parties across the spectrum (interview, Progressive Youth Alliance (PYA) leader, 12 February 2015). While this tendency constitute the erosion of intra-party democracy and it is well known within the political circles, there seems to be no or limited practical measures undertaken to contain its escalation. That there is no concrete action to end the unethical conduct which is characteristic of the relations between political parties and their allied-student movements and youth wings is analogous to the uncertainty of the future of democracy in South Africa. This should be worrying for all South Africans across the political divide. Hence, the erosion of democratic practices within political parties constitutes an overall threat to the sustainability of democracy in the country. This claim is guided by the general understanding that political parties are the key stakeholders for democratisation in the country and if its broader democracy is to be sustained, it ought to be rooted from within them.

While it is true that some student movements' capacity to influence developments within political parties is at times compromised by external forces, it is also correct to state that such movements are in certain instances also hesitant to rally behind and offer real support to certain potential candidates who did not rise within their rank and file. More importantly, student movements without an *umbilical cord* attached to a particular party often find internal resistance from the general membership in its quest to influence the content and direction of the leadership of any given political party. In the same vein, the membership and leadership of established parties often do not accept nomination of potential candidates by student movements who are not affiliated to them. There is no gainsaying that the cauldron of the mixture of factors that incapacitate or disinterest student movements to be actively engaged with internal party dynamics to ensure real youth representation in the candidate lists of political parties robs South Africa of the wealth composite of new ideas, actions, values and victories.

The failure of the student movements to correct this abnormal situation within South Africa's political parties was well captured by the legendary Mphahlele (2002: 6-7), when he asserted that "[T]he South African ruling class believes innovation is equivalent to opposition – which it does not allow". Although, it may be difficult to find lasting solutions to the triple challenges of unemployment, poverty and inequality, the first step in this journey should be to stop the exploitation of student movements to serve narrow and selfish interests of individual political leaders or political party factions.

Concluding remarks

The aim of this Afrocentric chapter has been to present and examine the role played by student movements in ensuring that youth are included as potential candidates in the electoral lists for democratic South Africa's political parties. Despite their limits in forwarding and/or seconding youth candidates for political parties' electoral lists; the fact that non-political student movements (i.e. fees must fall movement) are powerful and can alter the political agenda of South Africa towards a particular direction cannot be denied (Buys, 2016). It is on this basis that in certain circles, their genuine cause and activities have been deliberately described as a reflection of the work of the so called "third force" (Mancu, 2016). For this author, the characterisation of the non-political 2015 national student movement as the element of the "third force", which seeks to engineer regime change in South Africa is devoid of truth. That "the doors of learning shall be opened to all", across the colour and class divisions have found expression in the anti-colonial/apartheid rhetoric of many countries including South Africa (Khapoya, 2010; Shai, 2013). Such a commitment has been legislated in the new democratic dispensation (Republic of South Africa, 1996). As such, it is politically, morally and historically justified for any student movement in South Africa to advance calls for "free education".

In the final analysis, the cessation of the exploitation of student movements for sectional interests is possible when fundamental principles such as 'representativeness, openness, democracy and independence' find true and honest expression within such networks (Proteasa, 2002). This is an ideal situation which will re-affirm the relevance of student movements in both party and national politics. It will also give currency to Nelson Mandela's (2015) illustrative message to the nation that "[Y]ou, the young lions (youth) have energised our entire struggle". Flowing from this, it is the careful conviction of this chapter that student movements can also influence political parties to include the youth in their lists through an intense and sometimes adversarial process of political bargaining. This bargaining happens when movements forward their preferred names to parties for consideration. This is never a straightforward process, it can take many months to resolve. What we see is that the student movements do have the political clout (bargaining muscle) to bargain with political parties when it comes to candidate selection.

References

African Youth and Governance Conference (AYGC) Initiative. 2015. *7th African Youth and Governance Conference*. Resolution Booklet. 9-15 August 2015. Accra: Youth Bridge Foundation.

Asante, M.K. 1990. *Kemet, Afrocentricity and Knowledge*. Trenton: Africa World Press.

Asante, M.K. 2003. Afrocentricity: *The Theory of Social Change*. Chicago: African American Images.

Badat, M.S. 1999. *Black student politics, higher education and apartheid: From SASO to SANSCO, 1968-1990*. Pretoria: Human Sciences Research Council.

Buys, R. 2016. A student convention can avert revolution. *Sunday Times*, 13 March 2016.

Djanie, A. 2016. The trouble with money. *New African*, Vol 558: 32-33.

Isaak, A.C. 1985. *Scope and Methods of Political Science: An introduction to the methodology of political enquiry*, (4th ed.). California: Brooks/Cole Publishing Company.

Khapoya, V.B. 2010. *The African Experience-An Introduction*. New York: Longman.

Kivilu, M., Davids, Y., Langa, Z., Maphunye, K., Mncwango, B., Sedumedi, S. & Struwig, J. 2005. Survey on South African voter participation in elections. Report prepared for the Independent

Electoral Commission (IEC). Pretoria: Human Sciences Research Council (HSRC).

Mafisa, L. & Mtati, N. 2009. Preservation of African traditions and encapsulation of Moral Values as part of African Indigenous Knowledge. Paper presented at a conference on "Revitalising African Value Systems for Sustainable Continental Integration: Perspectives from Emerging Scholars", Johannesburg, 25-26 June 2009.

Mancu, X. 2016. A chink in the ANC's armour. *New African*, Vol 558: 28-31.

Mandela, N. Freedom looms large on the horizon. *The Star*, 11 February 2015.

Mashayekhi, M. 2001. The Revival of the Student Movement in Post-Revolutionary Iran.*International Journal of Politics, Culture and Society*, 15 (2): 283-313.

Mbeki, T. 2010. The role of Africa's student leaders in developing the African continent. https://www.uct.ac.za/usr/news/lectures/misc/mbeki_SLS.pdf (Accessed 12 February 2015).

Mkabela, Q. 2005. Using the Afrocentric Method in Researching Indigenous African Culture.*The Qualitative Report*, Vol 10 (1): 178-189.

Modupe, D.S. 2003. The Afrocentric Philosophical Perspective: Narrative Outline. In Mazama, A. (Ed).*The Afrocentric Paradigm*. Trenton: Africa World Press.

Mphahlele, E. 2002.*Es'kia*. Cape Town: Kwela Books.

Mpumelelo, M. 2011. Crass liberalism is the new culture. http://www.sowetanlive.co.za/columnists/2011/11/02/crass-liberalism-is-the-new-culture (Accessed 13 February 2015).

National Youth Commission. 2002. *Status of the Youth report*. Pretoria: Government printer.

National Education, Health and Allied Workers Union (NEHAWU). 2016. *Higher Education Sector Bulletin*, April 2016. Johannesburg: NEHAWU.

Nkondo, M. 2012. *Setting the platform for 2014 elections – Born frees learning from veterans: Talking about the future of fundamental change in South Africa*. Polokwane: Electoral Commission of South Africa.

Owusu-Ansah, F.E. &Mji, G. 2013.African indigenous knowledge and research.*African Journal of Disability*, Vol 2 (1): 1-5.

Proteasa, V. 2002. Pillars of the student movement. In Oye, O., Jungblut, J. &Chachava, K. (eds). *The Student Union Development Handwork for a Stronger Student Movement.* Brussels: European Students' Union.

Ramose, M.B. 2002. *African philosophy through Ubuntu.* Kadoma: Mond Books.

Republic of South Africa (RSA). 1996. *The Constitution, Act 108 of 1996.* Pretoria: Government Print.

Scheurich, J.J. & Young, M.D. 1997.Coloring Epistemologies: Are Our Research Epistemologies Racially Biased? *Educational Researcher,* Vol 26 (4): 4-16.

Schulze-Herzenberg, C. 2014.*Voter participation in the South African elections of 2014.*Policy Brief. Pretoria: Institute for Security Studies (ISS).

Shai, K.B. 2009. *Rethinking United States-South Africa Relations.*Hoedspruit: Royal B. Foundation.

Shai, K.B. 2013. *A Revised Student Guide to African Politricks: Selected Essays.* Sovenga: University of Limpopo.

Thaba, K.T. 2016. Repositioning the United States of America's foreign policy towards Cuba: changes and continuities under Barack Obama's Administration.Unpublished BA Hons mini-dissertation.Sove 9781913976002nga: University of Limpopo.

Tracey, L. 2016. Corruption at the highest level: will the ANC maintain voter confidence? *ISS Today,* 11 April 2016.

Vuma, S.L. 2013. *The role played by Turfloop student activism in the struggle against apartheid.* Turfloop: University of Limpopo.

Welsing, F.C. 2015. The Cress Theory of Colour-Confrontation.*The Black Scholar,* Vol 5 (8): 32-40.

A

Africa Institute of South Africa, 16, 30, 31, 47, 48, 61, 62, 78, 79, 80, 111, 144
African National Congress, 128, 129, 142, 149
Afrocentricity, v, ix, x, xi, xii, 18, 19, 23, 28, 35, 43, 45, 50, 51, 58, 59, 65, 66, 67, 75, 76, 77, 85, 95, 101, 105, 110, 111, 113, 114, 115, 116, 117, 118, 119, 120, 121, 122, 123, 124, 129, 130, 131, 132, 141, 142, 150, 156
Asante, Molefi, viii, ix, xii, 18, 19, 28, 34, 35, 36, 42, 43, 45, 51, 59, 65, 66, 67, 68, 72, 76, 80, 85, 95, 101, 103, 105, 110, 111, 113, 114, 115, 117, 118, 119, 121, 122, 124, 125, 130, 131, 132, 142, 149, 150, 156
Azanian People's Organisation, 140

B

Batalea Publishers, 16, 20, 27, 31, 50, 65, 79
Black Economic Empowerment, 136
Botswana, 58, 135
Burke, Edmund, 90, 130, 131, 142, 146

C

Cabral, Amilcar, 34
Chikane, Frank, 22, 28
Clientelism, 153
Communist Party of South Africa, 133, 140
Constitution of the Republic of South Africa, 1996, 135
Council on Higher Education, 73, 77, 102, 110

D

Department of Higher Education and Training, 22, 70, 105, 108, 110, 144
Disruptive pedagogy, ix
Duncan, Jane, 105

E

Economic Freedom Fighters, xiii, 144, 149
Education Policy Consortium, 134, 142
Euro-Americans, 113, 120, 123
Eurocentric intellectual onslaught, viii
Eurocentric value system, 86
Executive Dean, 93

F

Faculty Research Professor, 93
Freedom Charter, 133, 142

G

Ghana, 31, 48, 58, 62, 80, 97, 125, 145
Goebbels, Joseph, 36
Gordon, Lewis, 70

H

Higher Education Transformation Network, 87, 91, 92, 96, 103, 108, 110
Historical Association of South Africa, 58

I

Independent Electoral Commission of South Africa, 147
International Conference on Public Administration and Development Alternatives, 16, 43, 50
International Institute of Applied Systems Analysis, 68

K

Kangaroo courts, 104
Knowledge imperialism, 58
KwaZulu-Natal, 55, 138

L

Limpopo Province, xiv, 87, 144

M

Madzivhandila, Thanyani, v
Mandela, Nelson, 135, 156, 157
Manyaka, Rasodi K, 16, 23, 26, 29, 44, 46, 50, 54, 60, 122, 124
Maserumule, Mashupye H., 17, 21, 22, 23, 24, 26, 29, 33, 40, 42, 46, 47, 50, 59, 60, 61, 65, 66, 69, 70, 72, 78, 86, 96, 113, 114, 120, 121, 124, 125, 130, 143
Mazrui, Ali, 46, 83, 124, 127, 144
Mbeki, Thabo, 41, 47, 134, 137, 144, 146, 152, 157
Mokaba, Peter, 151
Mugabe, Robert, 113
Munzhedzi, PH, v

N

National Development Plan, 69, 79
National Education, Health and Allied Workers Union, 88, 147, 157
National Institute of Humanities and Social Sciences, xiv, 58, 68
National Party, 57, 140
National Programme of Political Literacy, 152
National Research Foundation, 57, 68
National Student Financial Aid Scheme, 134
National Youth Commission, 149, 157
Nigeria, 58
Nkuna, Nghamula, 28, 30, 37, 47, 58, 60, 61, 71, 79, 135, 141, 144
Nyawasha, Tawanda Sydesky, viii, ix, xii, 60, 86, 95, 97, 113, 114, 115, 116, 117, 118, 119, 120, 121, 122, 123, 125, 126, 153
Nzimande, Blade, 101, 111, 129, 141

O

Okri, Ben, 21

P

Pan Africanist Congress of Azania, 121, 140, 153
Phahlane, Khomotso, 129
Phahlane, Phahlane, 143
Political Science, 27, 33, 49, 63, 75, 99, 106, 120, 156
Politricks, 36, 42, 63, 98
Popular Movement for the Liberation of Angola, 133
Progressive Youth Alliance, 154
Public Administration, xiv, 16, 21, 22, 23, 28, 29, 30, 31, 33, 38, 42, 43, 46, 47, 49, 50, 55, 60, 61, 63, 65, 71, 72, 74, 77, 78, 79, 96, 97, 99, 121, 124, 125, 143, 144, 145

R

Ramaphosa, Cyril, 90, 97, 151

S

School of Development Studies, University of Mpumalanga, Mbombela, South Africa, v
School of Management Sciences, University of Venda, Thohoyandou, South Africa, v
Sebola, Mokoko, viii, 15, 23, 24, 35, 46, 49, 52, 55, 60, 66, 77, 83, 97, 99, 113, 145
South African Association of Political Studies- Limpopo Chapter, xiv
South African Association of Public Administration and Management, xiv, 16, 29, 42, 50, 78, 144, 145
South African National Qualifications Framework, 72, 80
South African Post-Secondary Education, 55
South African Students Organisation, 151
Student Representative Council, 150
Students Representative Council, 100

T

Tambo, Oliver, 139, 140
Theology, 25
Tiro, Onkgopotse Abraham, 151
Tourism Studies, 25, 50
Traore, Karim, ii

U

Ubuntu, 84, 86, 152, 158
University of Cape Town, 138, 143, 152
University of Johannesburg, 105, 138
University of Limpopo, 16, 29, 31, 32, 48, 50, 62, 73, 77, 78, 79, 80, 81, 87, 96, 97, 111, 125, 138, 143, 145, 150, 151, 152, 158

University of Pretoria, 93, 135

V

Vice-Chancellors, 100

W

Westernised epistemology, 114
White social history, 150
Wilson, Woodrow, 27

Y

Young Southern African Scholars Program, 68

Z

Zuma, Jacob, 97, 126, 139

www.ingramcontent.com/pod-product-compliance
Lightning Source LLC
Chambersburg PA
CBHW071940240426
43669CB00048B/2479